D0584612

"Where spiritual warfare is taken seriously, it is often experience-driven rather than scripturally based. Yet many of the rest of us, especially in the West, think very little about Satan and demons. This is a rare book that I, for one, will read again and recommend to others."

*Dr. Michael S. Horton*
*Host of whitehorseinn.org*
*Editor in chief,* Modern Reformation *magazine*

"Relatively brief, but captivating. A perceptive investigation. Ideal for an older youth or adult Bible study group. Easy, engaging style—as if the author is speaking directly to his readers as he insightfully leads them through many different scenarios and situations."

*Dr. Ernst R. Wendland*
*Lusaka Lutheran Seminary, Zambia*

"It's about time! Our Western culture has shrugged at and belittled this topic for too long. This book helped me measure and reassess our family's alertness to demons and Satan's deceiving ways."

*Amanda Rose*
*Founder of holyhenhouse.com*
*Wife and mother of three*

"It expanded my perspective on the presence of demons and their impact on our everyday lives. I believe that the insights gained from this text will help me to keep my skepticism in check and to consider the impact of Satan's demons on the future patients that I will treat as a physician."

*Adam Miller*
*Medical student, Medical College of Wisconsin*

"A very valuable work. It is a beautiful devotional that a Christian can use in all times of trial and struggle. Definitely an eye-opener."

*Prof. Gaylin R. Schmeling*
*President, Bethany Lutheran Theological Seminary*

# 2000 DEMONS

## No Match for My Savior

### Jesus' Infinite Power Over Evil

E. ALLEN SORUM

**NORTHWESTERN PUBLISHING HOUSE**
Milwaukee, Wisconsin

Second printing, 2018

Cover illustrations: iStock Photo and Shutterstock
Art Director: Karen Knutson
Design Team: Sarah Messner and Lynda Williams

Northwestern Publishing House
1250 N. 113th St., Milwaukee, WI 53226-3284
www.nph.net
© 2016 Northwestern Publishing House
Published 2016
Printed in the United States of America
ISBN 978-0-8100-2777-0
ISBN 978-0-8100-2778-7 (e-book)

# TABLE OF CONTENTS

# FOREWORD

By Pastor Pheng Moua

As a refugee from Southeast Asia, I grew up learning and embracing the tradition of my ancestors. The spiritual realm is always something that clouds the minds and hearts of my people. Most of us fear the unseen spirits. We imagine they eventually will swallow us up slowly, like a snake devouring its crushed prey. We know our community is surrounded by demons. We are afraid. We don't want to talk about it. We fear that by talking about demons, they will take over our lives and souls. Evil spirits are real and dangerous.

By the Lord's grace, I was called out of this spiritual darkness into his wonderful light and now serve as a minister for Christ. I have seen and known people saved from the grip of the devil's hands by a demonstration of the Lord Jesus Christ's mighty power. When the gospel first reached many of my people, they refused to believe it without a demonstration of its power. The name Jesus Christ is a powerful name. I have seen Jesus' name deliver and save many people from the devil, and these people, in turn, were brought to accept Jesus Christ as their only Savior.

This book covers the wonderful ministry Christ came to do, which is to destroy the work of the devil. This book provides information that will strengthen Christians—not to fear but to be diligent, watchful, and ready to fight the devil at all times. The author encourages the readers that Christ has already overcome the power of darkness and rescued them from sin. In Christ, we can stand firm and have no fear of the devil. Christ will fight for us.

I want my people to have this information. It will be so good for them. Yes, it will help them understand how demons want to torture people. But more than that, they need to be informed about how Jesus works through his Word to rescue people. My people need to know as much as they can about the power of Jesus. This book shows how Christ uses his power to rescue his people. I want my people to have this insight for fighting their spiritual battles, so that together we can have the victory.

I also think the Christian community at large needs this book and needs to realize the spiritual warfare we all are experiencing. We need to understand the consequences of this warfare. It is real, and we need to be ready to face it. This book will help us be ready. It equips all Christians to prepare for spiritual battle and to live godly lives as we wait for the Lord Jesus Christ's return.

# PREFACE

*"[Moses] persevered because
he saw him who is invisible."
Hebrews 11:27*

I hope that reading this book will open your eyes
to what you cannot see. "See" Jesus, your Savior.
"See" demons and the devil, your adversaries. Then,
seeing more clearly the unseen, you will lift your
voice in praise to Jesus for guarding you from these
enemies. And, finally, I hope your time here will make
you want to raise your arms in prayer to Jesus to
continue his watch over your soul.

How am I qualified to engage anybody on this
topic?

I am not an exorcist.

As the director of the Pastoral Studies Institute of
Wisconsin Lutheran Seminary, one of my main tasks
is to train men from various ethnic and immigrant
backgrounds to serve as pastors in the Wisconsin

Evangelical Lutheran Synod. In working with spiritual leaders from different countries and cultures, I have had to learn to "see" some things that I had missed before. Christians, coworkers, and students from places far and near have brought me into their experiences with the spirit world. I have not dealt directly with demons or the demon-possessed. I am not looking to change that. But my job has required me to support those who do deal directly with demons. In the process of helping, I have had to adjust my own thoughts and perspectives on the spirit world. My coworkers have been patient with me and have taught me. I am eager to share with you a few of their stories and their important insights on the matter of dealing with demons.

I am even more eager to share with you the written record of Jesus' experience with demons and the devil. The Bible offers exactly the eye-opening power necessary to accomplish the purpose of this little book. We will look at Mark's gospel especially, together digging into Mark's narrative of the day when Jesus performed his biggest exorcism. We will see that this was quite a day for the small band of disciples whom Jesus had just recruited to follow him. This day will be special for us too, as we relive it.

Does it seem to you that, generally speaking, the activity of demonic forces is growing in our world? Are we more aware of demon activity or are demons just more open and bold these days? Their influence seems to grow. Many lives are ruined. This does not need to be. We have access to power that rescues people from demons. We have the power to keep people safe from demons. May our time together in the pages that follow bring us closer to that power!

# CHAPTER
# ONE

*"Your enemy the devil prowls
around like a roaring lion
looking for someone to devour."*
*1 Peter 5:8*

Before we begin to unfold and reflect on the events of this dramatic day in Jesus' life, please let me ask: Do you believe in demons? Do you believe in the devil? Are you persuaded that the devil and his demons want to hurt you? Are you worried about demons and maybe even afraid that you could run into one? If you did run into one, how would you recognize him? (or her? or them?) What do you think?

Perspectives are wide-ranging.

Let's start with Robert's view.[1] His pockets bristle with devices that track activities and manage information. He gets together with friends and coworkers to talk about technical topics. One matter that has never come up in any of his personal or professional circles is the potential threat of demons. He would not consider legitimate the idea that demons come from some spiritual place in a spiritual form to bring suffering on humans. Sickness is spread by germs. Robert would tell you to wash your hands often and be well! He would be impatient with anyone trying to dodge responsibility by accusing outside forces for bad outcomes.

Dawb—she prefers this traditional name to her English name—is the oldest child of immigrant parents

[1] "Robert" and the three persons that follow are composite characters I will use to illustrate different points of view.

who came to North America from Southeast Asia. Dawb wants to be left alone. But there is no place she can go to be alone; spirits and their mischief are everywhere. Dawb hopes that her family, the ones who have died and passed into their next place, can protect her—at least a little. Lately, Dawb's father brings extra offerings to the small shrine in the family's home to secure the ancestors' assistance. Both of her little brothers are still sick. The family suspects that someone sent magic to cause this trouble. Tonight, finally, the healer will come to their home. And if the healer is not able to help, the family will have to bring the shaman in to deal directly with these spirits—or the magic. The shaman's fees are high, probably too high for the family to handle. Dawb's father and uncles meet to discuss strategy and options. Dawb's father is afraid. She sees it. She sees that her uncles are also afraid. This makes Dawb afraid.

Jenny's view on things supernatural is connected to her social life with high school friends. For instance, Jenny goes to parties. One of Jenny's friends who comes to the parties is learning how to "do readings." These readings come out of creepy cards she deals out to her friends. The girls squeal when someone gets the "tower" card. If you get that card, it means your boyfriend will drop you for sure. "Ask the cards anything! They show you the future." Jenny wonders about that. How can turning over a card reveal or direct the future? Anyway, once people start playing it, the game takes over the party. Everybody wants answers, and there is always "just one more" question to ask.

Let's add Jonathan's perspective to this list. Ghosts are his hobby. He likes to read about houses and their poltergeists. These spirits, in Jonathan's view, do not represent evil or want necessarily to harm humans. He believes that every ghost has a story, almost always a tragic one. Ghosts like this, he is sure, give off an aura. By measuring different kinds of energy, their presence can be confirmed. They can be summoned. Communication is not only possible, it is the desired outcome. Jonathan is not at all sympathetic to religion's view that these are evil demons. He eagerly seeks a relationship with the paranormal.

There are definitely more perspectives, but this conversation is already getting crowded. Robert is skeptical. Dawb is fully engaged. Jenny finds it all a source of entertainment, an icebreaker. Jonathan wants an interface with the supernatural. But here is the reason I have written out these descriptions—and this is my heartfelt prayer: I want you, please, to think about your own perspective. Which of these viewpoints do you most connect with? Any? Does one of them resonate? Do you ever discuss the world of spirits, demons, the supernatural, the paranormal, or the occult? If so, what are those discussions like?

Full disclosure? I get Robert's disinclination to even consider the existence of demons or that they may have any impact on my everyday life.

I think back to conversations I had with American Indian spiritual leaders. They shared their encounters with "skin walkers." A Navaho told me about a nighttime car ride into the reservation. As he drove along at normal highway speeds, an Indian spirit ran up alongside of his car. "The skin walker turned his face to me, smiled, and ran off into the darkness. I was scared, man!" The story over, I remained silent. I waited for a punch line or a moral to the story. I did not think that he was serious.

Not many days after hearing the sprinting skin walker story, I walked up to a group of several American Indian men conversing on a street corner. After some preliminary small talk, I asked the men whether they had had any experience with this phenomenon of skin walkers. My impudent curiosity almost got me into trouble! Their body language morphed into menacing. Simultaneously, each member of the group made it clear that my fact-finding mission had crossed some kind of line. One of them threatened me physically. Before they could organize the promised thrashing, I ran. That's right. I ran. It seemed the prudent thing to do.

Over the years and up to now, bizarre accounts of personal encounters with demons and spirits have infringed upon my worldview. The people who tell me these stories know that it is with some risk they share them with "outsiders" like me. The risk I speak of is that someone like me, from where I come from, could very easily reject the story and discredit the teller. I appreciate very much that I get to hear these stories and that people are willing to risk telling them to me. But the stories still challenge me—a little. As I travel and make new friends in different cultures and places, I know that I will hear more stories. Sometimes, if the stories seem slow in coming, I ask. And when I ask, the accounts come— accounts with incredible details that challenge me.

I believe the stories that I hear. Or I believe that I should believe them. Part of me wonders, "Who can I tell this story to back home that will not think me naïve or silly for believing it?" Maybe the challenge is not with the stories I hear away from home, but with the reaction I anticipate when I tell these stories back home. I project my own skepticism onto my family and friends. Obviously, therefore, I should be reluctant to retell the incredible accounts of personal encounters with demons and spirits to my mainstream, Western, "skeptical" community back home. Yet sometimes I cannot hold these stories back. They boil over and out like a pot of rice on the stove. Depending on the company I am with and the circumstances at hand, in a moment of weakness, I share a bizarre story of a personal encounter with the evil of demons. But here is a surprise: I am not ridiculed. The account is not rejected as fancy, myth, or primitive superstition.

Then I wonder, what is my problem? Why do I harbor even a particle of skepticism? I wonder if you would bump into the same reaction. If you were to admit to your friends a regard for or concerns about the spirit world, would you discover not skepticism but perhaps an awkward curiosity? You might encounter something between a conviction and dread. One thing that helps me to let go of some of my lingering skepticism about the demon world is that I just do not meet very many skeptics. But I know I have much more skepticism to let go of. I want to grow out of it completely.

Are you a "Robert" like me? Can we make this journey together?

But this book is not just for the Roberts.

As I have said,[2] I work on a close personal level with many Christians from other cultures who cannot understand how anyone could struggle with doubts about the spirit world. Like Dawb, these Christians would consider such skepticism dangerous, yes, irresponsible. On the other hand, Dawb's conviction encroaches upon obsession. Her burden is a sense of helplessness over against a malicious presence that eludes human control. More than half[3] of the people from Dawb's immigrant community in North America rely upon a shaman—a witch doctor—to intercede for them when circumstances suggest that the spirits are unhappy.

When a shaman cannot mediate successfully for the suffering family member, Christian pastors are sometimes called upon to serve—often out of a sense of desperation. The pastor accepts these terms. A team of members of the congregation soon arrive to offer prayers and encouragement. It is soon evident that these are not friendly spirits. For communities like this who are fully—woefully—engaged in the spirit world, the question is not, "Do spirits exist?" The question is, "How can we possibly be safe from them?"

---

[2] In the preface.

[3] This is the figure given by members of that immigrant community.

Is that the question you wrestle with? This book will show you it is a wise question to ask. But, believe me, there is an answer. I will help you see it. I will help you find encouragement in it.

People like high school Jenny and ghost whisperer Jonathan would not follow Robert's rationalized rejection of spirits. Jenny's and Jonathan's views represent a cohort of American culture that has a serious interest in spirits, ghosts, the supernatural, and the occult. This slice of North American culture is "fully engaged" with the spirit world, though not in Dawb's way. Evidence of a wide interest in the spirit world lies in the fact, for example, that horror films in America have earned more than 8.3 billion dollars in one ten-year period.[4] America's film industry responds to this interest by producing between two hundred to three hundred new horror movies a year. Many are rated PG-13.[5]

I admit with some embarrassment that I missed the whole "Jason" and "Freddy" craze.[6] The trailers alone scared the daylights out of me. I bought a ticket for a horror movie just one time in my life. I did not make

[4] www.the-numbers.com / market / genres

[5] Apparently the producers of horror movies count on parents' willingness to allow their children to support the industry.

[6] Jason was the main character in *Friday the 13th* movies. Freddy was the main character in *A Nightmare on Elm Street* movies.

it to the end of the movie. I couldn't handle it. I was terrified and traumatized even before all the characters had been introduced onscreen. That movie's images of occult horror and demons are as clear in my mind right now as they were 30 years ago when I was sitting—briefly—in the movie theater.[7] Call me a scaredy-cat but I am not the only one who has a hard time sitting through horror flicks. A lot of us do not process this form of "entertainment" well.

Horror movies are popular in many countries. There is also an international market for music that explores occult themes. Bookstores offer horror literature and occult fiction. Check the best sellers right now: more than one will have an occult-related theme. Clothing and makeup styles associated with the occult are sold, and not just in specialty stores. Or would you like to dress up as the devil or a witch next Halloween? No problem. Amazon offers about one hundred different versions of Ouija boards, including a pink version for girls. Are these family-friendly board games for fun and entertainment?[8] You can find a Tarot card reader

---

[7] I suppose this is one way I am not like Robert the skeptic either: For him, a movie about demons and horror is just as unreal as one about giant flying dragons or superheroes.

[8] Even a professional poltergeist researcher (Dale Kaczmarek, www.ghostresearch.org/articles/ouija.html) suggests that the Ouija board is not just a game.

in your city. YouTube videos will show you how to conduct séance table tilting. Human interest in the world of spirits and the occult fuels a portfolio of these "entertainment" industries.

Forces and images and ideas that some cultures want to escape are regarded as entertainment by others. Which cultures are acting more wisely?

Science is also interested in the supernatural. Want to earn a degree in paranormal research or paranormal psychology? You will not have any trouble finding an academic or professional institution to help you earn that certification. You could even pursue a PhD in parapsychology or the like. Go on a study tour to investigate ghosts. Purchase single access EMF meters[9] to measure paranormal activity. Learn how to apply the scientific method to the supernatural. From Jonathan's perspective, there is no room here for skepticism or religion or fear.

But what is the nature of the supernatural? Is there any problem with the paranormal? Are you afraid of it? Should you be afraid of it? Is it evil? Is it bad, immoral, wicked? What do you think? Is Satan a character for a child's Halloween costume? Or is he a dangerous

---

[9] EMF meters measure variations in electromagnetic fields.

enemy who wants to possess us and destroy us? If you are not sure or think not, you hold the majority view. Most people in North America do not think that the devil is real—in the sense that he is a personal being intent on evil. Even only 25 percent of those who identify themselves as Christians are of the opinion that Satan is a real and living being intent on hurting people.[10] If the devil and demons and the spirit world are not threats to our souls and to our eternal destiny, then why would it be a problem for us to spend billions on horror films and do ghost research? We can acknowledge a spirit's existence as long as we harbor no presumptions as to its character. We must not test the spirits—apparently.

Again, the reason I have spent all these words describing these different perspectives is to get you to think, "What's my perspective on demons or the spirit world? How real or how malicious or how dangerous or how harmless do I actually think demons are, from one day to the next?"

What if your perspective on the spirit world is seriously wrong?

---

[10] www.barna.org/barna-update/faith-spirituality/260-most-american-christians-do-not-believe-that-satan-or-the-holy-spirit-exis#

Is there even one objectively right perspective, that is to say, a perspective that is "best" for people like Robert, Dawb, Jenny, Jonathan, and for you and me? If we acknowledge that these creatures are real, can we figure out what they want? And if what they want is to hurt us, is there any reliable way to get help against them?

What if the best perspective on the matter of spirits and demons is that of the writer of the gospel of Mark from almost two thousand years ago? His detailed reporting of the day of Jesus' biggest exorcism teaches us a perspective on the spirit world that I want to believe. It is not yet my perspective, completely, but I want it to be. It is this: *If not for the constant protection Jesus of Nazareth has given us up to this very moment, the demons would likely have us all naked, screaming, bleeding, and living in burial caves.*

## Study Questions

Which perspective on demons could you most relate to? Or would you like to add another to the list? Explain.

When was the last time you had a conversation about demons or the spirit world? What was the conversation like? Was it a comfortable topic for you to raise?

What's the difference between believing in the existence of demons and taking their existence seriously?

"Even only 25 percent of those who identify themselves as Christians are of the opinion that Satan is a real and living being intent on hurting people." What do you think of that statistic? What has led to it being such a small number?

Have you, or has someone close to you, ever encountered a demon? How do you know? Did this person recognize this encounter as potentially dangerous or threatening?

Describe how your perspective on demons is changing so far, or how it isn't changing.

# CHAPTER
# TWO

*"'My name is Legion,' he
replied, 'for we are many.'"*
*Mark 5:9*

The soft sand grabbed the bottom of the boat. On shore! The disciples scrambled out of the boat. Finally, they could exhale. Soaked and shivering, just tying a knot in the line was a chore. What just happened?

A moment—or forever—ago, a hurricane wind pounded them. Huge swells threatened to drown them. Meanwhile, the teacher, Jesus, slept in the stern! Panicked disciples shook Jesus out of his slumber. "Jesus," they screamed, "we are going to die and don't you care?" What did they think Jesus would do? What could he do? The secret question they were wrestling with was, "What are we doing out here in the first place?"

Jesus opened his eyes to the wide eyes of cowering "professional" sailors. Raising himself into the face of the wind, he commanded, "Silence! Be still!" Had Jesus rebuked the weather? And had the weather obeyed? Then, suddenly, everyone was ashore and unharmed. Such a close call!

Back on solid ground, they felt safe. But while securing the boat, they heard a shout: "Jesus!" Today everyone had been yelling the teacher's name. This time, though, the voice was unfamiliar; it did not come from Jesus' crew. It came from where? that hill? Or, more precisely, from that pale figure sprinting down the hill toward the landing party. The disciples squinted to focus on this darting ghost. Emaciated and battered, his color matched the dirt of the hills. Naked, filthy, and frantic, the man was as threatening as a rabid beast. How could this gaunt shell produce a noise powerful enough almost to wake the corpses in the tombs he just escaped? Like a cowering dog, the man gathered himself at Jesus' feet and sneered, "Jesus, Son of the Most High God, what do you want with us?" The disciples wanted to jump back, but they were trapped on a narrow strip of sand, pinned between the sea and this creature at Jesus' feet. Arrogant in spite of his naked, filthy frame, the man demanded again, "What's your business here, Jesus? You didn't come to torment us?"

One minute, a storm like they had never seen. In the next minute, a man like they had never seen. Would he tear them limb from limb? Dried blood was under his fingernails. They cowered. Their panicked eyes searched for the teacher. And there was the teacher. Look at him. Fearless and calm. Had he been expecting this confrontation? It was like Jesus had written his own script for today: "Calm storm. Land boat. Meet lunatic."

Jesus studied the man kneeling before him. What was Jesus studying? What did he see beyond a miserable lunatic? In that same voice the disciples had just heard over the howling wind—a powerful voice, a trumpet blast loud over the clash of battle—Jesus said, "Come out of this man, you impure spirit!" (Mark 5:8).

"Come out of this man." Jesus was not talking to the man. Looking past or through the wounds and the dirt, past the dark and sad eyes, ignoring the person—the human being—on the ground, Jesus spoke. To whom? Or maybe we should ask, to what? The disciples soon found out. "What is your name?" Jesus asked. "Legion," he said—because many demons had entered him. Jesus was speaking to *Legion.* That name, the word, hit the disciples hard. They knew of Roman legions, thousands of strong and mighty men marching in full battle readiness. Thousands of men, maybe six thousand men with six thousand shields, swords, and spears with six thousand breastplates declaring solidarity under one flag that had never fallen. But the Legion that Jesus was speaking to, the thousands of strong soldiers of darkness who had just heard their new orders, was inside this man. Jesus had just commanded thousands of demons to come out of one man, one human being.

## Was This Truly a Case of Demon Possession?

Stop! Back up! Do you have a problem with this scene? I might. There is a voice in my head, and the voice whispers, "No, actually, Jesus was not speaking to thousands of demons but to one broken, dirty, lunatic of a man." I hear the voice of Robert the skeptic inside me, and that voice is having a hard time with the idea of thousands of spirits—a legion of demons—in one man. I have to ponder what I think of this chief demon, representing thousands of fellow demons, inside a man in preliminary negotiations with Jesus.

The voice explains it away: "Jesus was just acknowledging the lunatic's incorrect self-diagnosis that he was demon-possessed." Yes, something like that. Jesus was playing along with the man. The man, poor fellow, just thought he was demon-possessed. Maybe he was actually afflicted with some physical issue, malnutrition, or sleepless nights—any of which could produce demonic self-delusion. Jesus' command, "Get out!" was therapy. The therapy rescued the man from his nightmares. Like a psychic chiropractor, Jesus adjusted the brother's misaligned brain so that "healed" he could leave the gloomy caves and return to his home, to his family, and to his career.

The voice, unchallenged, grows bolder: "Perhaps Jesus was himself under the assumption—popular in that primitive generation, closely held in that backward community—that this mentally distressed man was demon-possessed." Jesus, you see, was also under the delusion that demons were the cause of this man's suffering. But delusion won the day! Jesus'"exorcism" worked! The man lying face down in the sand mistakenly thought that he had demons. He heard Jesus order the demons out. So the man then (mistakenly) concluded that all the demons had departed from him. In spite of all the superstitious, tribal, backwater inanity, the right outcome was achieved. This would be a hardcore skeptic's explanation, would you agree? But let's consider it.

I think Mark, our gospel storyteller, anticipated some of this kind of skepticism. Mark's details do not leave room for it. His account and the accounts in the gospel records of Matthew and Luke do not allow our skeptical voices to blame on illness or ignorance what the accounts specifically refer to as "demons." To say that Jesus was accommodating himself to the man's delusion or that Jesus himself was equally deluded is to deny facts.

Mark reports that the demon-possessed man's neighbors had tried to restrain him. With the best technology of their day—chains on his hands and irons on his feet—they placed this man in bonds that would hold a man as strong as many men. But the demon-possessed man broke chains and smashed irons as easily as his mother used to snap kindling to restart the kitchen fire. No one could restrain this man. No bonds available to the people of this community could protect them from the violent attacks of the demon-possessed man.

Matthew's account mentions two demon-possessed men. Mark's and Luke's accounts focus on the demon-possessed man most involved with Jesus, the one who most engaged with Jesus. Matthew reports that these two men made it impossible for anyone to pass through the territory they controlled. An entire community would corroborate what Matthew, Mark, and Luke all stated clearly, namely, that these men were demon-possessed. The clearest demonstration of all was the fact that when the demons were allowed into the herd of two thousand pigs, all two thousand pigs rushed down the hill into the sea to self-destruction. The demon-possessed tomb dwellers were violent and powerful beyond human measure and beyond human control. The demons made them that way. Jesus did not address the man until he had cleared all the demons out of the man. These accredited and carefully presented particulars are meant to put our skeptical natures—yours and mine—to rest. Maybe Mark saw us coming.

Thousands of demons, a true legion of unclean spirits, took possession of one man's body? Can we set our skepticism aside long enough to consider what implications there are for us if the gospel writers are giving us the facts about this case? What would this mean for us? Anything? And what does any of this suggest about the urgency of a relationship between me and Jesus?

## A First Step Toward a New Perspective

Consider this imaginary scenario. We are on a battlefield. From our hiding spot, we can watch our enemy approach. He is bigger than us. He is better armed than us. He is victorious after a thousand campaigns with barely a nick in his armor. And behind this enemy marches a mad force of eager slayers just like him; this enemy never travels alone. They sniff the air as though they smell our blood. If we are discovered, we will learn in a hurry how inferior our strength is. And we will not just be crushed. We will be humiliated. These killers mock as they dismember. So what should we do? On the count of 3, let's cover our ears, bury our faces in our knees, and pretend nobody's coming.

I think probably not.

Go ahead and admit that the skeptic's voice— Robert's voice—makes us wonder. I know, personally, it is hard to grasp these ideas. It is hard for me to take seriously that such an army is, in fact, watching my every move, close enough to smell my blood. I'm not sure if I have ever taken it that seriously.

We do not like to think of ourselves as gullible or unsophisticated. We do not want to present ourselves that way to the world. We do not want to appear unsophisticated by not being able to join in on the small talk about popular books and movies that center on the occult. Young people do not want to appear or feel unsophisticated because they do not join in with high school Jenny to put their finger on top of a Ouija board or underneath a tilting table. We do not want Jonathan the paranormal expert to rebuke us: "I have dealt with spirits and poltergeists; they aren't so different from you and me. Don't fall for those popular misconceptions!" But it is not unsophisticated or misconceived to take seriously the threat of thousands of demons that are stronger than we are and would each fight for a turn at tormenting us. What would be gullible would be to think that if we only pretend they aren't real, they'll probably just leave.

Acknowledge the threat! See the enemy!

In a moment, we will see that we have one infinitely more powerful than this enemy and the threat these demons pose. Tremendously important encouragement is coming in just a few more pages. But before we celebrate how safe we can be, let's assess the true power and intent of the enemy.

The enemy is Legion. We need a word from our language and our culture that communicates to us irresistible power, force, skill, and sheer numbers in the same way *Legion* communicated that to the disciples and to the people of Jesus' time and place. What would that word be? I do not know if I have such a word. But the devil and his demons are tremendous in terms of their power and their number. Their appetite, their desire, their tireless plotting for our harm and humiliation is beyond our knowing; we cannot grasp it. Let our new perspective start here.

## Demons Are Unclean Spirits

The man who, hands and knees in the sand, bowed before Jesus was physical host to thousands of spirits. Jesus called these merciless trespassers "impure" or "unclean" spirits. For a Jewish person to be regarded or declared "impure" in the 1,400 years between Moses and Jesus meant that this person was not able to participate in the worship life of the community. It could also have meant that the person was not allowed to participate in Jewish community life. This was a ceremonial unfitness— a spiritual pollution or contamination—that required the unclean person to be separated from God. When Jesus called these spirits unclean, he was declaring them unfit for any kind of friendship or association with God or with humans.

By any standard and by every measure, these demons were unclean spirits. The spirits drove this man into graves carved into the side of a hill. Touching any dead thing would make a Jewish person ceremonially unfit to be with God or with the community. People from a Jewish background, trained in the requirements of ceremonial rituals, would abhor contact with any-thing dead. They would be especially offended by the idea of living in tombs. But who would not be? Living among dead bones and decaying bodies suggests something very unclean and very unnatural.

The demons certainly were unclean. They were not fit to be friends with God or with humans. Look what they did to the person whose body they possessed! The demons ripped clothes off their victim. The demons ripped chains off their victim. No decency, no bonds, no shackles, and no chains could restrain the demons in this demon-possessed man. With superhuman strength, these unrestrained bullies attacked innocent neighbors who had not learned to avoid the tombs. Unable to escape and unable to run away, these passersby were beaten by the fists of a man who could not control the impulses of the demons that brought those fists upon his neighbors. There was no way for one human to restrain the thousands of unclean impulses of thousands of unclean demons. The demons were the unclean ones, but the activities they forced their host into made him unclean too, unfit for fellowship with God or people. The man certainly endured physical pain. But did it compare to the shame and isolation and self-loathing that the demons forced upon him? Demons are not content to be unclean themselves. Their desire is to make everything and everyone they touch repulsive, unapproachable, and shameful to God and to people.

The writers of the gospels saw with their own eyes how the terrible demons treated their victims. They saw the terrible outcome of being possessed by unclean spirits, namely, isolation, impurity, shame, loneliness, depression, and humiliation. The writers of the gospels want to show us—God wants to show us—the true nature of demons. This is what demons do to people. They possess people in order to oppress them in every way possible. Jesus called them unclean spirits. That description still fits demons, who are still seeking to possess us.

*Possess* is a good and accurate word in this instance. Observe their behavior. See what they do. They seek to own us. Once they have possession of us, their will is not to protect us as you or I might want to protect a possession. Not demons. Their will regarding the ones they possess is to humiliate, to hurt, and, finally, to drag into eternal judgment. Hell is the demons' destiny. Demons know it, and they work hard to drag humans into it.

### A Perspective: Do Not Make It Easy for Demons!

Back to our perspective now. What is a good perspective? Is a new one taking shape in your heart and mind? Is the skepticism of Robert getting quieter inside you? Is the curiosity of Jenny and Jonathan turning into a sober vigilance? There are a lot of perspectives out there regarding demons. But a really good perspective starts off by "seeing" the demons and by "seeing" and acknowledging and completely grasping what these unclean spirits want to do to us.

A good perspective is challenging. It will not be easy. Evaluating and assessing how I may be making it too easy for demons to deceive me will not be easy. But in view of the facts, I think I should do it. Do you? What are we doing that may be making it easy for demons to begin to control us, own us, and ruin us? Do we regard too highly our own strength? Do we minimize the demon's intent? Is there any chance that our adventures are becoming addictions? These are not easy questions. An unclean world of evil and violence and games invites us: do we see the extreme danger? Let's cover our ears, bury our faces in our knees, and pretend the danger isn't there. No! Think what demons do. Jesus called them unclean. It's who they are. Do you see it?

Most days, I don't see it. It is not real to me. A thousand pairs of ancient eyes, watching me. If they had their way, I would be a naked, screaming lunatic that no straightjacket could hold. I would be cruel to every passerby. My favorite place would be a crypt. I don't pray like that's real, like that's the danger I'm in. I don't praise Jesus for keeping me safe from all that.

How real is it to you?

Is the danger really that great? Are the demons really all that vicious?

## The Fear That Motivates Demons

The man was on his knees before Jesus. In a sense, not literally, the demons were too. Mark's account has the demons begging Jesus to grant this plea: "In God's name don't torture me!" (5:7). In Luke's account, the demons explain what they meant by "torture": they kept on begging Jesus not to send them into "the Abyss" (8:31). Matthew tells us the demons also asked Jesus a question: "Have you come here to torture us before the appointed time?" (8:29).

What sense would the disciples have made of the demons' begging?

They had learned in Sabbath school: the demons follow—or at least once followed—their head, the devil. The devil is the chief unclean spirit. He is the "god of this age" (2 Corinthians 4:4) and the "prince of this world" (John 12:31) who rewards his subjects with a darkness that keeps them blind to the glory of God's love. At first the devil and the demons were among the holy angels, the "clean" spirits, created by

God to serve God's people (Hebrews 1:14). But they rejected their proper place and function.[ll] The devil organized them in a rebellion against God that resulted in many angels being "swept . . . out of the sky" (Revelation 12:4). These rejected angels were flung to earth. The devil and demons are spirits just as the angels are spirits, traveling throughout the earth just as the angels do. At the same time, the devil and demons are held in spiritual chains, weighed down under the darkness of God's wrath, even while they rule over the earthly kingdoms of this world.

The early torture and the Abyss that the demons begged Jesus not to cast them into are references to their final judgment on the Last Day. The devil's kingdom of this world will become the kingdom of our Lord (Revelation 11:15). Satan and his demons and all those who insist on following the devil's ways will be confined forever to the lake of fire and sulfur to suffer (Revelation 20:10).

Demons cannot escape their chains! Demons cannot escape their ultimate doom. What an incredibly encouraging truth, as well as an important contribution to our perspective!

---

[ll] Jude 6 and 2 Peter 2:4

But until their future doom comes, God—for his own unfathomable reasons—allows the devil to spread enmity, to roam the earth, and to deceive those who have rejected God's love. Satan hurries because his time to hurt humans is short (Revelation 12:12). A powerful and vast army of terrible enemies is unleashed on this earth to hurt us. They cannot unleash themselves from their chains. They cannot escape their destiny. But they are like roaring lions in search of prey (1 Peter 5:8). They are not lazy killers. This is why the demons did not want to be sent "early" to their final torture in what will be the Abyss of the burning lake of condemnation. They wanted every moment that could be called theirs to torment humans.

The devil and his demons just do not want to be destroyed alone. Their nature, their corrupt and unclean character, finds great satisfaction in bringing all of us into their destruction—yes, and by bringing tears to the eyes of God. Jesus once preached about the rejoicing that goes on in heaven when one sinner repents (Luke 15:7). So what is the emotion in heaven when sinners do not repent? Not long before he died, Jesus wept over his own people in the city of Jerusalem because, he said, "You did not recognize the time of God's coming to you" (Luke 19:44). The devil delights in every precious soul he can lead away from God. In this way, God is robbed of the fellowship that he wants with every person. The devil and his demons are unclean, for sure.

To speak of the devil trying to get back at God by stealing souls away from God is a very religious conversation. We are discussing good and bad motives with good and bad eternal outcomes. We are talking about where you and I will spend eternity!

There is a contradiction in present times regarding the spirit world. On the one hand, the Christian religion, the pursuit of absolute truth, and the concept of objective morality (that is, what is right for me is also right for you) are quickly losing ground. On the other hand, interest in spirits, ghosts, the supernatural, and the paranormal is gaining. For many, interest in spirits has nothing to do with how humans should live their lives on this earth in relation to other humans or where humans might spend eternity when they die. The current interest in spirits seems to testify to a human craving not for God or for a peaceful conscience but for adventure. Interest now in the spirit world and the supernatural is about new experiences and new relationships.

Does that seem like a good perspective to you?

What if the gospel of Mark is right? What if spirits and demons are not phenomena? They are personal beings from an evil, unseen world that have an agenda. They share a purpose. They—and we are speaking of many thousands of them—want to hurt and humiliate humans. Yes, the only "joy" that remains for them, so far as I can see, is to vent their anger against God by waging war against what God cherishes most, namely, human beings.

Are you a human being? Then you are at great risk. The demons want to wage war against you. They want to destroy you. How is that for a perspective? It is not a cheerful perspective. But it is an important one!

How can it be that we are not destroyed already? If the enemy is so evil, so numerous, so strong and determined, how is it possible that I am not crushed already? Is there someone I should be saying a thousand thank yous to for this?

And why would I dare to do anything that would make it easier for my enemy to move upon me and into my heart and soul? If I call upon this enemy to guide me or gain something for me or even to entertain me, how long before he attends to me? And will he come alone or by the thousands?

## Will We Encounter Demons Today?

Where would you expect to encounter a real live demon today? How far would you have to travel? What obscure or remote or hidden culture would you have to explore? With even a little bit of research, you might find that you do not need to travel far at all. For most of us, I would venture that a trip across town would allow the opportunity to meet people who are in direct contact with demons. A business card posted on a bulletin board at a truck stop 15 minutes from my house gives the contact information for paranormal investigators. Their website offers "to prove or disprove the validity of paranormal activity in everyday environments" and "to give peace and comfort to persons living with the fear of the spirits."[12]

North America's growth is driven by immigrants. Your new neighbors from distant lands may have been raised in religions that have called upon demons for generations. Do you remember Dawb in chapter 1? As I said, she is a composite character. But everything about her is real, a combination of many true stories I have heard from working with immigrants from Southeast Asia. A key concern of ancient religions is

[12] www.tricountyparanormalgroup.com

how to get spirits on our side and keep them there. The Christian faith is making inroads into these communities because the old ways of negotiating with demons do not help.

I have been to other lands where the demon-possessed roam openly in their misery. I stood on a street corner in one of these places with my friend from there. We watched a person on the other side of the street who was in a difficult situation. I asked my host to explain the situation in front of us. He replied, "The man is probably possessed." The register of my host's voice suggested that what we were watching was not unusual in his experience or in this town. A visitor might not at first recognize demon-possession. The people who live there do. That skeptical voice inside may again take issue with the logic of "those simple foreigners." That voice would argue that a person who chooses to live on the streets in any place is probably dealing with mental health issues. But sometimes evidence before you suggests that the diagnosis of mental illness is insufficient. I can tell you more about that evidence later.

We can wish that there were no more unclean spirits possessing human victims. We do not want to think that such a great misfortune could befall anyone . . .

or us. But wishing it away won't help. We must keep working on a new perspective that acknowledges what is both an ancient truth and a present truth: unclean spirits possess people.

People do not need an ancient or foreign religion to call upon the devil and demons for assistance. The devil will rush to any call for help or guidance. Call on the devil and he will come. It is not possible to make it any easier for the devil and his demons to discover you than for you to call out his name and ask for his help. But his assistance comes at a price. The devil's rule is in this world. He will use his power, make available his resources, and give freely of everything that this world has to offer. The devil controls the world's resources, but they are meaningless to him. He is a spiritual being. Physical riches are only valuable to him for the reason that he can use them to gather humans into his congregation of the dead, the spiritually dead. He will gladly exchange his world's wealth and pleasure for you. Demons delight in open invitations. How could they not? Whether through Dawb's traditional religion, through Jonathan's paranormal "research," or through Jenny's naïve choices for entertainment, the demons will rush in when summoned.

Or if, like Robert, we cover our ears and insist that demons do not exist—or that if they do exist, they are harmless creatures who just want to be heard—the demons are just as pleased with this perspective. For we are thereby left with no protection.

Demons operate as openly among humans as humans permit. Were we to offer our hearts and minds to demons with such a no-strings-attached invitation, they would jump on it with both of their "impure" feet. Invite them. They will come. What could be more predictable? In domains where traditional religions have called upon demons for generations, one must be careful not to trip over them. To that extent, Dawb's perspective is accurate: they are everywhere.

## What Do We Do First?

We want a perspective that does not make it easy for demons to attack us. We begin to achieve that perspective simply by acknowledging that the devil and his demons are out there and they want to hurt us.

In this chapter, we began a journey. Is there a place called Sheepish? There must be, because that is where I am. I feel like I have no place writing a book like this, because so often I've been the one burying my face in my knees.

I need a better perspective on all of this. I humbly invite you to work with me on this. The best perspective is taking shape. So far, it is sounding something like this: Jesus, you have somehow guarded my heart! My proud thinking overestimates my strength and diminishes the devil's danger. Open my eyes to my real enemy and my only enemy.[13] Teach me to value my present and eternal safety even as you do by resisting the devil so that he will flee from me.[14] The devil and his demons are a powerful force of unspeakable evil determined to destroy me. I begin each day not fearing but acknowledging that fact. For by acknowledging that fact, I can only seek security and protection in One more powerful than the devil and demons.

There is One more powerful than demons, even thousands of them. We have security and protection in the One who is powerful and willing to save. You will see that he saves. You will see how he saves. You will see what Jesus already demonstrated on a sandy shore in Galilee.

---

[13] Ephesians 6:11,12. In these verses, the apostle Paul makes clear that "flesh and blood" is not our enemy, but our enemies are Satan, the demonic dark powers, and the spiritual forces of evil.

[14] James 4:7 promises just this.

## Study Questions

What point made in this chapter most impressed you with how "unclean" demons are?

In your own words, what are the "chains" that the demons are wearing now?

How well did this chapter's arguments respond to someone like Robert the skeptic? Do you feel the book is treating the views of skeptics with the proper amount of understanding and respect? Explain.

What is the difference between obsessive fear of demons (like in Dawb's culture) and the perspective this chapter is advocating?

Describe a time when you felt some of the uncleanness that you read about in this chapter. What are some healthy, positive ways of coping with these feelings? Who might you talk to? What could you do if you do not have a person to help you through these times?

Respond to the following comment: "I have grown up as the son of a pastor; however, I identify with Robert in this book. Despite my knowledge on the subject, translating Bible knowledge/history/faith into the real world is a challenge for me and always has been. How could demons such as Legion actually be out there trying to attack me? As a 30-year-old man,...I believe that 'Roberts' are 95 percent of the population of people in my demographic (white, middle class, Christians and non-Christians). I believe that this book being written from a 'recovering Robert's' perspective reaches me specifically."

Describe situations into which we might put ourselves that could make us vulnerable to the attacks of demons. Are there times or circumstances in a person's life that might increase their vulnerability to demons?

# CHAPTER
# THREE

*"The reason the Son of God appeared was to destroy the devil's work." 1 John 3:8*

Who knows what compelled Jesus to do some of the things he did?

John's gospel reports that, earlier in his ministry, Jesus "had to go through Samaria" (4:4). Who said Jesus "had to go through" this land that the Jews, Jews like Jesus, most always avoided? The Samaritans were distant cousins of the Jews. The Jews of Jesus' day looked down on them because they had given up their commitment to keep their Hebrew heritage pure. But as you read through that chapter of John, you see that Jesus was compelled to make that journey to bring God's good news to a woman whose lifestyle had alienated her from her community. And when she heard this good news, she made sure that the very community that had isolated her was invited to hear it for themselves. Jesus "had to go through Samaria" because he had to do the will of his Father, to bring faith to new communities. And Jesus would not let the bigotry of his day keep him from his obligation.

I think Jesus "had to go through" the stormy sea the day he met Legion for the same reason: to bring someone faith, to bring good news to a gentile (non-Jewish) demon-possessed man. Jesus had to get to this shore because he knew the suffering of the man whom thousands of unclean spirits had invaded. Indeed, there was a script. Right now we are at the part that read, "Deliver lunatic."

As for those unclean spirits, there can be no stronger proof of their uncleanness than their plea for mercy. How can that level of pride and hypocrisy be measured? What mercy had these wicked allies of Satan ever demonstrated to their human victims? The demon-possessed man had spent his nights among dead bodies, his days in isolation, and his life in naked humiliation. The demons delighted in torturing their human victim in a brutal, relentless, and shocking manner. Now these spirits of squalor wanted Jesus to show to them a Savior's tender heart? This was pure hypocrisy! Showing the arrogance that got them kicked out of heaven in the first place, the demons used the name of God to try to force Jesus into showing kindness: "In God's name don't torture me!" "Legion," that is to say thousands of demons, begged Jesus to allow them to remain in this remote graveyard haunt rather than be sent early to their place of eternal confinement. Then they turned to the herd of pigs. "Send us into the pigs," they begged. The demons were begging Jesus for a favor. They appealed to the Savior for a break. Amazing. Unmerciful demons sought mercy from the One who is more powerful than demons.

Just before landing on this shore, the disciples had asked one another about Jesus, "Who is this?" (Mark 4:41). What kind of man was Jesus? The demons knew the answer. They knew what kind of man he was. That is why they submitted to him at the shoreline as they did. They brought themselves low before the Son of God, who had been sent by the Father to destroy their hold on the hearts of men and women. Jesus was, they knew, the more powerful one—the one who ruled over them and the one who controlled their immediate and eternal fate. And if only to escape an early condemnation to their final and eternal fate—hell—they begged Jesus for a break.

The demons did not come to Jesus with repentant hearts, confessing sorrow over past acts of rebellion. Did this awful crowd of unclean thousands actually believe that Jesus might show them kindness? That is a hard question. Regardless, in their dread of Jesus' power, the demons were not too proud to beg for consideration. But demons begging Jesus for an act of openhanded pity and generosity inspires another question: Do I really expect kindness from Jesus when I shout out his name?

## Jesus Rescued You!

Patricia was a new Christian and a new member of the church where I served as a pastor. Just before Christmas, Patricia asked me to visit her mother, who was nearing death. I visited her mother every day for several days. I shared with her that she did not need to fear death because Jesus had won eternal life for her by his perfect life and by his suffering and death on the cross. Very early in our conversations, Patricia's mother would grant that Jesus was the Savior of the world. But she refused to confess, "Jesus is my Savior." I did not immediately understand how this frightened lady could confess that Jesus was everyone's Savior except hers. I asked her why she could not acknowledge or confess or believe that Jesus was her Savior too. Finally, she confided in me. She said, "I am not worthy."

On Christmas Day, the day before Patricia's mother died, she did confess, "Jesus is my Savior." Before that day, Patricia's mother knew about Jesus. She knew what kind of man Jesus was. But that is not enough. Finally, by the power of God's Spirit, through the sharing of the Christmas story, a little frightened lady crossed over from trembling guilt to unshakable hope, from knowing about Jesus to believing in Jesus, from knowing what kind of man Jesus was to what kind of Savior Jesus is . . . for her.

I know I am not worthy. In desperation I just might call out Jesus' name. I might even yell it. But are my cries for mercy, at bottom, just as proud as the demons' cries? What do I "see"? Do I see all of my past acts of rebellion? Goodness knows my rebellious acts are as numerous as Legion—beyond Legion. Sometimes I feel like the "I'm sorry" I say to Jesus is too fake. But there is something else for me to "see": a Savior who came a very long way to rescue me!

Jesus came to this world to bring mercy to humans. However alienated you may feel from the church, from your loved ones, from God in heaven, right now I beg you to believe that Jesus came all this way, to planet Earth, for you. The eternal Son of God took on human flesh to walk this earth, to keep God's commands, and to suffer hell on the cross for everyone in the world—and for you. You are not excluded from mercy. Jesus pleads with you to come and receive it. And in receiving Jesus, you receive the power of the most powerful One to rescue you from every evil attack of the devil and his demons!

### Demons Enter Two Thousand Pigs

But what about that herd of pigs? Have you ever wondered why a herd of pigs might be rooting and relaxing so near to a people for whom this animal was unclean? A Jewish person who followed Old Testament ceremonial laws would not manage a pig herd and surely would not eat pig flesh. The Jewish person following Moses' Law would not try to sell pork to his people because there would be no market for it. Pigs were unclean. So how could there be a large herd—two thousand pigs—available for the demons to rush into?

Jesus had directed the boat to the eastern shore of the Sea of Galilee, to the region of the Gerasenes, close to the ten cities known as the Decapolis. This was Gentile land, the home of various tribes and peoples who were not Jewish. It would not have been unusual for these Gentiles, that is, non-Jewish people, to raise pigs. A herd this large could have been a community co-op. A typical family in this time and place would not have enjoyed the resources to gather or to manage such a tremendous asset. Perhaps this herd of two thousand pigs was the result of combining one hundred herds of twenty. A herd of two thousand pigs was already remarkable. That thousands of demons wanted Jesus to send them into that huge herd is beyond remarkable—it's crazy!

Jesus accommodated the plea of thousands of demons. Imagine the scene. Thousands of fleeing, screeching, angry, evicted demons rushing into two thousand unsuspecting domestic animals. With a lurch and convulsions that those tending the pigs could not explain, the poor animals rushed headlong into the sea to their deaths. What was the point of this? What was the point of the pigs rushing headlong down the steep slope into the sea? Imagine the magnitude of the loss. What could be more unclean than two thousand dead pigs floating out to sea or, worse, washing up onto the shore? What was the point of this?

Matthew, Mark, and Luke all report this destruction of the swine herd. None of them explains it or even comments on it. The writers of the gospels simply report that Jesus sent the demons, according to the request of the demons, into the pigs. The pigs then sprinted into the sea to their destruction. Every one of them drowned. Why? We are given no explanation.

How can we comment? What explanations or speculations might we offer since the Bible prefers to be silent on this topic? What the reader sees in this account is that Jesus is able to order thousands of demons away with a simple word.[15] Never before had this world seen such power over the spirit world! It

---

[15] The act itself demonstrates and illustrates the truthfulness of John the Baptist's announcement: "After me comes the one more powerful than I" (Mark 1:7).

also seems fair to suggest that because everything we have seen so far about demons shows their lust for mindless, cruel devastation, the ruin of the pig herd emphasizes the character of demons. The damage demons do shocks us; it takes our breath away. Demons delight in depraved demolition of all things decent and all things living. If demons can destroy anything that God values or loves, watch them: they'll do it.

The destruction that demons desire is put on display by their plea to enter into two thousand helpless livestock. And immediately upon entering them, the demons drive them into the sea. The disciples who shortly before this event feared drowning in the sea now watched crazed swine pitch themselves into the sea. The disciples stood there and watched two thousand pigs drown. What comments could they offer? What speculations could they propose? Thousands of unclean spirits drove "unclean" pigs to their deaths. Point made. No comment necessary. This is just the kind of thing demons do; it's their character.

## What Jesus Values

Against this backdrop of absurd, mindless, costly destruction by unclean spirits, now see Jesus. Jesus is not yelling. Jesus is not begging, carrying on, or negotiating self-serving treaties. Jesus, first of all, is in this scene because he wants to help and to serve and to save. This is what Jesus does. This is why Jesus came to this earth. This is why Jesus came to this shore.

Jesus demonstrated his superior power and also his generous character when he gave a simple order to the demons: "Come out of this man!" It was a quick exorcism. The demons departed. Jesus' order was executed. Jesus speaks; the universe responds. Earlier in the day, Jesus restored calm on the sea. Now on shore, Jesus restored calm in a man's life. With a word, a man was saved from demons—thousands of them. They left. Jesus is powerful. He is more powerful than demons. He is more powerful than the wind and sea. He uses his power to display mercy to suffering humans. There could not be a more severe disparity than the character of demons compared to the heart of Jesus.

Jesus allowed the demons to destroy the pigs. We can only guess why Jesus allowed the destruction of what was the property of others—but his creation. What we do not need to guess at was how Jesus felt about the man who was the previous host to these thousands of demons. Jesus' actions spoke more than clearly. Jesus was absolutely opposed to allowing the demons to destroy this man. Jesus rescued the man. The purpose of this trip was accomplished. Who knows the monetary value of the pigs? How much were they worth? Who knows why Jesus allowed the demons to destroy them? But we know exactly how much this man was worth. Jesus sailed across a stormy sea to save one suffering human soul. Jesus journeyed to this land of Gentiles to save this Gentile. And there was also this Gentile's friend, remember? There were two whom Jesus so valued. He came to this unclean place along the eastern shore to save two suffering souls. We know the value Jesus attached to these two men. They were precious.

Do you suppose the disciples were catching this? As they looked back upon the events of the day, were they learning what Jesus wanted them to learn? And in this moment right now, are we learning what Jesus wants us to learn? What is the best perspective regarding demons? What are we thinking right now about our perspective on the spirit world, over which Jesus is Lord, Ruler, Master, and King?

## A Perspective: Jesus Is Powerful for Me

Sometimes I do not feel worthy to cry out to Jesus to rescue me. Sometimes, and this is painful to admit, I lack confidence in Jesus to respond to my cry. How could I possibly think for a moment that my Lord Jesus would not rescue me? Yes, that sounds ridiculous and blasphemous, especially after we have seen the power and love and saving character of our Savior Jesus.

The fact is, one of the main points throughout all of Mark's gospel record of Jesus' life and ministry is the hard hearts of his disciples. In the gospel according to Mark, there are arguably 11 episodes[16] in which Jesus rebukes the slowness of the disciples to believe. These are the "hearts hardened" that Jesus rebukes and that Mark points out again and again. Why would Mark make the blindness of the disciples a major theme in his gospel? I personally think that, though it is difficult for me to acknowledge, God has given me Mark's gospel to see my own frail faith condition in the blindness of the disciples and the other characters I read about here. God has given us Mark's gospel to help us acknowledge our own hard hearts. More important, we see in Mark's gospel a Savior's heart that is patient and forbearing, a Savior who will walk with us until our hearts spill over with confident faith in him. The best perspective gives us eyes to "see" Jesus as the powerful one, always ready for and worthy of our call for help. This confidence and firm resolve is his gift to us.

---

[16] Passages where Mark refers to the disciples receiving correction or reproof include 4:13; 4:40; 6:52; 7:18; 8:17-21; 8:33; 9:33; 10:14; 10:42-45; 14:37,38; 16:14. There seems to be an implied rebuke or an opening for one in 5:31; 6:37; 8:4; 9:32; 10:32; 14:31; 14:72; 16:11-13.

Our resolve to trust Jesus is meant to grow every time we see Jesus' character and kindness in action. Jesus came to this earth to rescue humans. Jesus traveled throughout Palestine to rescue thousands of hurting people. Jesus helped his own tribe. Jesus helped people from different ethnic communities, including those whom people from his culture looked down upon. Really, I would say the main purpose of the whole gospel of Mark is to show us this powerful Son of God who came to rescue people—to rescue you.

What if I forget how much I need a powerful rescuer? I forget how much I need to call upon Jesus because of the unclean enemies around me. I forget to count on him, to trust in him as all that keeps me sane and safe and tolerable enough for anyone else to come near me or love me. I need his patience at least as much as I need his power.

## Driving Out Demons Today

Still today, Jesus shows his patient and loving desire to rescue people from unclean spirits.

A pastor who serves in my church body lives in one of those distant lands I mentioned before. He serves people who suffer from demon possession. Most of the members of his congregation first came to him because they or family members sought help from demon possession. In his efforts to help, this pastor has encountered demons. The evidence that they are actual demons makes it foolhardy to deny them. In his ministry to the demon-possessed, my colleague encounters voices. The voices are not ones that the possessed person has ever used. There are various voices and various personalities behind the voices. It seems demons still do not like to live alone inside their human hosts. The voices reveal things and share things that the possessed person would not know. As the pastor prays next to the possessed person, strange things happen. Frightening things happen.

My purpose in bringing this up is not to make you afraid of the demons who still today possess our fellow human beings. I am only setting the stage for what happens when this pastor encounters these demons. I want to try to express in a convincing way the amazing ministry that this pastor, whom I also consider my friend, carries out in the face of frightening forces. I am in awe of his courage, his faith, and his love. All of these are required in deep measure for him to sit in a room alongside a person out of whom strange voices and even stranger words gush forth. But in this pastor, see the Savior at work. See the Savior's heart still in action, saving and rescuing hurting humans. My pastor-friend is called upon often to go to homes to pray alongside the bruised and hurting. This pastor goes out of his way. He goes often. He goes until there is no need to go anymore. And he goes to pray.

This pastor and the people he takes with him into these situations go when families come to them for help. Usually, the family of a demon-possessed person comes when no one else or nothing else has managed to deliver the demon-possessed person. This pastor may be a family's last hope. The family does not come to the pastor knowing that he can help. They are desperate. They think just maybe this pastor and his prayers *might* help. These are the terms. The pastor accepts them. He will go to pray and will try to help.

My pastor-friend encourages me—and helps my perspective on the spirit world—not just because of what I would describe as his courageous faith but also because of his sincere humility. This pastor insists that he has never once cast out a demon. That sounds strange when you think about the fact that most of his members came to his church and came to the Savior because they were rescued from demons through his prayers. But he insists that he has never cast out a demon and that he would not even try.

He prays. When he is asked to help someone who thinks that he or she or a loved one has an unclean spirit, he will go to that person and he will pray. My friend calls upon Jesus to cast out the demons. When the demons leave, the pastor reports to the family that "Jesus removed the demons." Jesus gets the glory. Jesus ordered the demons out. Jesus is the powerful one. Jesus is the one in charge.

Pastors like this one and their people have helped me to develop a proper and right perspective on demons. These servants of Jesus have encountered too many demons to either deny them or to be overly impressed by their frightening behaviors. At the same time, they know that they must prepare for these encounters. Even with confident faith and sincere humility in place, even with a process that calls upon Jesus to remove the demons, this praying with and for a demon-possessed person is a perilous undertaking. Truly, the demon-possessed person needs prayers. It is just as true that the people praying with and for the demon-possessed need prayers.

We have already seen the character of demons in Mark's account of the casting out of Legion. Demons show this unclean character even now. During the prayers of the Christians who are calling on Jesus to remove the demons, the demons will try to shame those who are praying by reporting past sins. Sins no one saw—no one but the invisible eyes that always watch from the shadows. Sins dredged up, now shouted in the hearing of all present. The demons want to chase off the Christians with shame and embarrassment: "Who are you to try to remove me?"

I do not know why God allows the demons to make public the sins of these Christians. Just like I don't know why he allowed the demons to kill all those pigs. Perhaps it is because he wants us to know for sure these are real enemies. Or he wants us to have no doubts about how very unclean these spirits are.

I have not asked my friends who do this work to take me along on an exorcism call. I am not curious to know how these voices sound or what they say. I would be more terrified of what past sins they would reveal about me to my coworker friends than of the voices themselves. If for some good reason I were asked to accompany such a ministry team, I suspect I would go. Yes, I will go. But it is not as though I need to see this thing.

When these pastor-friends of mine carry out this ministry, they do not engage in conversation with a demon. I do not need to have that experience either.

Who would negotiate with a demon? Why negotiate with the side that lost? We do not negotiate with losers. We do not give concessions to the vanquished. They lost. Jesus won. Jesus is the most powerful one who always wins, especially when it comes to demons. Jesus, you remove the demons! Removing demons is what Jesus does. Let it ever be so. No negotiations! In the name of Jesus, demon be gone!

Here is the good news: We do not have to negotiate with demons. Demons are in no position to negotiate with us! We know exactly what kind of man Jesus is. He is the God-man who came to this earth to defeat the devil and to protect us from his evil attacks. Because we belong to Jesus and because Jesus is ours, we are completely safe.

## Making My Pastor-Friend's Perspective My Own

My friend models for me the best possible perspective on demons: the perspective that is built upon Jesus Christ—our Lord and Savior—who has defeated the devil and will not allow him to deceive us anymore. This perspective looks not to ourselves but to our compassionate Lord and powerful Savior. We are weak, the demons are strong, but our Savior is stronger! We want to recognize he is near. We want to keep him near.

What would my life look like if this were my perspective day after day?

Every day I would pray, maybe even pray with the same intensity my friend has when helping the demon-possessed. Why not with that intensity? The demons that wait to prey on me and harm me are just as unclean and stubborn as those my friend faces.

I would keep the name of Jesus on my lips, not because it is some magic talisman but because I know how his name must frighten these unclean enemies of mine. My favorite Bible passages, snippets from my favorite hymns or Christian songs, lines from favorite prayers or sermons or the catechism—I would keep these on my lips and in my mind.

> The devil is called the master of a thousand arts. But what shall we call God's Word, which drives away and brings to nothing this master of a thousand arts with all his arts and power? The Word must indeed be the master of more than a hundred thousand arts. And shall we easily despise such power, profit, strength, and fruit? [17]

[17] Martin Luther, The Large Catechism, Longer Preface, par. 12,13. *Concordia: The Lutheran Confessions*, edited by Paul T. McCain, 2nd ed. (St. Louis: Concordia Publishing House, 2006), p. 354.

I would be on my guard against my pet temptations, with constant prayer to Jesus to give me victory
over them.

I would work to strengthen this perspective by
returning to the stories and promises in the Bible that
show my Savior's power against the fallen angels. I
would meditate on these. I would talk them over with
fellow Christians.

I would cling to the promises God gave me in
Baptism[18] and retreat often to the comfort and
courage God gives me through the Lord's Supper.

Perhaps most of all, I would be so thankful. I would
give more credit to Jesus than to my morning cup
of coffee for my clear head each day. "Thank you,
Jesus, that I had the sense to get dressed today before
I left the house. Thank you that I am not living in the
cemetery tombs. Thank you that I am not destroying
myself and everyone who comes near me. Thank you
that I have my wits about me. Thank you that the
unclean spirits do not rule my life, my mind, my soul."
I would praise him with all my voice for being my
powerful Guardian.

---

[18] We will discuss the relationship between Baptism and victory over demons more exten-
sively in chapter 5.

I would, I would, I would, but I don't. Not often. Not much. Not yet.

Will you pray for me? I am praying for you, to my Savior who knows everyone who will read this book.

He is patient, and he is praying too.

## Study Questions

God could certainly drive out a demon without people coming to pray for the possessed person. Why do you think prayer is so important in an exorcism? Why has God decided to drive out demons through the prayers of fellow Christians?

Why do you think Jesus allowed the pigs to be destroyed by the demons? Explain why you think this detail might be important to someone.

Should we ask questions like, "If Jesus loved this man so much, why did he allow the demons to ruin his life in the first place?"

What impresses you in this chapter about the power of Jesus?

How has this chapter added to your perspective of demons? of Jesus? Explain.

Is it a sin if I never thank Jesus for protecting me from demons? Why or why not?

Could you relate to the story of Patricia's mother? How?

# CHAPTER
# FOUR

*"Then the people began to plead with Jesus to leave their region." Mark 5:17*

Men had been hired to watch over the large herd of pigs. How many men does it take to lead two thousand pigs to good feeding grounds and to protect them from predators? That job would seem to require a team of several. Some of the men who were tending the pigs may have been close enough to Jesus to observe his conversation and maybe even overhear it. We can be confident that even before the conversation happened, when the demon-possessed man sprinted out of the tombs toward Jesus, the pig herders were on edge and vigilant. They were certainly aware of this dangerous man with the superhuman strength and the violent nature. Would we be unfair to expect that one of these pig herders might have tried to warn Jesus and his disciples about the danger they were in? Or, seeing that there was no opportunity to provide warning before the demon-possessed man charged the landing party, might one of the pig herders have called his partners near, saying, "We'd better be ready: those guys on the shore might soon need our help"?

I will be careful not to judge too soon or too harshly, since I was not present for the amazing events that all happened within moments of Jesus stepping on shore. But I have some suspicions about the character of these pig herders. Let's assume the pig herders watched the disciples land the boat. They surely heard the screaming demon-possessed man and watched him bull rush the landing party. If the two thousand demons were like their counterparts whom Jesus had cast out in different parts of Palestine, the demons probably screeched and hollered again in a terrifying display of defeat on their way out of the man and into the pigs.[19] There is no doubt that the herders watched their two thousand pigs cast themselves into the sea to drown. Mark's account also seems to suggest that the pig herders stood around long enough to see what had happened to the demon-possessed man.

Up to this point, I hope you would agree that we have been making fair assumptions. Maybe less likely, but might we also assume that there was at least the possibility that one or more of the pig herders knew the demon-possessed man before he had been possessed? Maybe they were once neighbors? But even if none of the pig herders knew the demon-possessed man personally, why would none of them walk over to the man and celebrate with him his new condition? There was no more work for them to do watching pigs. The pigs were gone. They had time on their hands.

---

[19] Mark 1:26; Mark 9:26; Luke 9:39 offer examples of screaming demons.

They watched thousands of demons exit this man in an incredibly dramatic fashion. They watched this man demonstrate his recovery by putting on clothes, sitting down calmly at Jesus' feet, and enjoying being "in his right mind" (Mark 5:15). If they were not interested in celebrating their neighbor's incredible recovery, would they not want to meet the man who achieved it? Admittedly, my case rests on assumptions. But it does seem to me our pig herders were light on character and lean on compassion.

The pig herders watched all of these incredible events and then ran off into the nearby towns and countryside to tell their people (and their employers?) that all the pigs just ran into the sea to their destruction and that the demon-possessed man had something to do with it. Part one of their report was, "Come and see what happened." Part two went, "It was not our fault!"

Agitated and intrigued by the breathless report of the swine keepers, the townspeople made straightway for the beach. Coming over the hill and looking down upon the shore, they saw Jesus. They saw swine carcasses floating out to sea or washing upon the shore. And remarkably, unimaginably, incredibly, they saw the demon-possessed man—the man who had oppressed them with his late night wailing and hard-fisted beatings—now sitting calmly at Jesus' feet, fully clothed, and in his right mind. Then the pig herders recounted the events from the point of the boat landing to the screaming demoniac to the charging pigs and, finally, to the restored man. The crowd listened. And then, for sure, the crowd turned to look at Jesus and to wonder, "Who is this man?"

### "Jesus, Go Away"?

Put yourself into that crowd which once stood upon the crest of the hill rising over the sea. Look down upon the scene. You might remember that demon-possessed man in a happier time. You might recall how you bump into his mother sometimes at the market. You know how many times you have thanked whoever controls your fate that you and your own children have been spared the ordeal of being taken over by demons. How many times had this beast of a man disturbed your sleep late in the night with his baleful wails? How many times had you wished that he would relocate to a different system of tombs? Maybe you had wished for a worse fate. But now you look down upon the scene alongside the sea. There this man sits, fully dressed and in his right mind. What do you do? What do you say?

The clear evidence in front of you declares, "Jesus is a powerful person who uses his power to help people and to do wonderful things!" Based on that evidence, what you probably would do is beg Jesus to stay. Or maybe if you were the mayor of one of these towns, you would give Jesus a key to the city. You would put him up in the most comfortable guesthouse and set up a triage for the homeless, the widows and orphans, the diseased and depressed. You would write up a list of good things that your town needs. You would point out the well that produces salty brown water and beg Jesus to heal the well. If you were a mother, wouldn't you beg Jesus to bless your children so that your offspring would never be invaded by bad spirits? You see what Jesus already did. What more could he yet do?

If you were in that crowd, the right thing to do would be to beg Jesus to stay. But that is not what the crowd did. They begged Jesus to leave. That was not the right response. That did not make sense.

Readers of Mark's gospel have asked why there were no complaints coming from angry pig owners. Why was there no inquiry as to the purpose of their herd's destruction? Or why was there no clamor about who was going to recompense the owners for the herd's destruction? But another reader might ask,

Why was there no celebration? A lost son had been regained. Peace and safety for their entire community had been restored. No more violence. No more howling. Why did they not gather around Jesus and the former demoniac and hug and dance and sing? They knew this man. He was one of them. They had known his torment. Now they could see his peace and wholeness. Close off the streets and have a region-wide celebration! But among this crowd, there was no joyful response of gratitude for a new future. There was only fear.

The crowd looked at Jesus and felt fear! Apparently they had not heard of his tender heart. They did not know his compassion. They had seen the outcome of his power over demons. They must not have trusted a mere man—as they viewed Jesus—with this much power. If only they had been just a little more curious. If only one of them had been bold to approach Jesus and to explore his nature. But it seems there was no bold or curious person in this crowd. They all agreed to ask Jesus to leave their community. They were afraid of Jesus.

The crowd could not have known this, but they should have feared the demons, not Jesus. After they killed the pigs, where did the filthy spirits go? These thousands of demons who had just been evicted from the body of their neighbor and who had just destroyed a herd of pigs were now homeless. They had no physical host to abuse and humiliate. But soon enough there was, standing upon a hill, overlooking that same sea, a crowd of empty hearts and vacant souls: a crowd of ready hosts. Ready for anyone but Jesus?

On another occasion, Jesus told the story of a demon that came out of a man and had to search for a new place to rest (Matthew 12:43-45). When the demon could not find a new place to rest, he returned to his former host. There in his former host, the demon found a room empty, swept clean and available. The demon invited seven more demons even worse than himself to join him in his refurbished home. "And the final condition of that person," Jesus said, "is worse than the first."

The thousands of demons who had just been driven out of the man from the Decapolis were not going to find a swept room in his heart for them. But did those thousands of demons find rooms ready and waiting for them in the hearts of the crowd of townspeople? I don't mean to imply that now instead of one man possessed by a legion, the whole crowd of townspeople had become possessed. But wasn't this a way that the demons could spread out, get comfortable again, and expand their reign of terror? Is this why the demons begged Jesus to allow them to remain in this region? For reasons not given to us, the people of this community at this point in their history appeared to prefer the dark demons they knew over the Lord of light who just arrived on their shores.

## Jesus' Response to the Crowd's Request of "Go Away"

I asked what you would have done if you had been part of the crowd. Now I ask what you would have done if you were Jesus. How do you think you would have responded to this timid and ungrateful crowd?

Think this through for just a moment from the perspective of Jesus. You had just traveled to a new community with a wonderful message. You had just endured the failure of your disciple "interns" on the stormy sea. You had just saved a man from thousands of demons and, with that act, also saved an entire region from the trouble and inconvenience of having a super strong, super violent demon-possessed person in the community. But now this community just wants you to go.

The disciples had remained silent throughout this episode. We do not know what they thought of this town's fear of Jesus and the people's request for Jesus to depart from them. There was another time, however, when the disciples did offer a suggestion when a community rejected Jesus. In that case too, the community that refused to receive Jesus was a non-Jewish crowd. Luke covers this account in his gospel.[20] Jesus wanted to pass through a Samaritan town on his way to Jerusalem. They sent Jesus away. The disciples wanted to call fire down from heaven to punish this unfriendly community of Samaritans. Jesus was not pleased with their spite, which the disciples attempted to veil with a concern for Jesus' honor.

At the risk of not pleasing Jesus again, fire from heaven would seem to me to be a perfectly appropriate punishment for this unfriendly crowd on that hillside overlooking drowned pigs and a healed neighbor. If I or if the disciples had anything to say about it, fire would fit the crime.

Jesus' heart is different. The Lord, the Bible wants us to know, is "patient with you, not wanting anyone to perish, but everyone to come to repentance" (2 Peter 3:9). The final judgment of the devil and all of his fol-

---

[20] Luke 9:51-56

lowers will come. But before it comes, before the Last Day, the Lord works to gather people into his church. I myself am proof of God's patience. We needed Jesus to be patient with us. Now we are his. Jesus will continue to gather his followers from every nation, language, tribe, and people right up to the end.

These are great truths that give us great comfort. Jesus is kind, tender, and determined to gather us into his eternal flock. Jesus is patient. His first impulse is not to send fire from heaven on every person that does not receive him immediately with faith and love. Jesus went to this region to rescue people. We know how Jesus would have wished the people to respond. We know this because we know Jesus' heart; he loves to help and to save. And I think we can predict how Jesus might have wanted this story in the region of the Decapolis to end. Go back to Sychar in Samaria for a moment. There we find a great alternative ending for this story from the Decapolis. Earlier we read that amazing passage in John's gospel: "[Jesus] had to go through Samaria" (4:4). Here is how that story ended. The woman who met Jesus at the well ran back to her fellow townspeople. She invited them to come and meet a man who just might be the Christ, the promised Savior. So this crowd of people from Sychar followed the woman back out to the well. Maybe they were curious. Maybe they really wanted to see if Jesus was the Savior of the world, the promised Christ. They begged Jesus to stay. Jesus stayed "two days" (4:40). In those two days, Jesus preached the good news. Many Samaritans became believers! Many Samaritans are in glory as we speak. What did the townspeople from the area of the Decapolis miss? Fear cost them a life-changing weekend with the Savior of the world.

## A Perspective: Believe Today!

So how did Jesus respond to this crowd from the region of the Decapolis? Ultimately, he honored their request. He got into the boat and left.

What should that say to us as we're trying to put together a perspective on demons and spirits? Is this a warning: "Don't look at the miracle Jesus did here the same way this crowd looked at it, saying, 'We'd rather not deal with this right now'"?

Our very best perspective sees that God wants our hearts today. He wants our devotion, not our delay. The new life that we want to live so that we can remain free from the deceit of Satan—will it begin today? Our praises and thanks and celebration of Jesus—will those begin again fresh and new today? Our prayers for our continued walk with Jesus—will those prayers begin with new vigor today?

It is proper for us to delight in the patience of our Lord. But it is also natural for us to test the Lord or try his patience. Why do I test God? I know I do. I put him off. I leave urgent matters for another time. I need to make changes. I still overestimate my strength against the devil and his ways. Or I am still too interested in the devil and his ways. Or, like the townspeople, I say, "This is all too big for me to wrap my head around right now: just let me go on with my life."

This is not what Jesus wants. Jesus has come all the way to you and to me. He invites us to join the man he freed from Legion. Sit with that man at Jesus' feet, enjoy Jesus' peace, and be safe. He calls to you, "Come to me, all you who are weary and burdened" (Matthew 11:28).

Will we come to him? listen to what he says? see him for who he is? welcome and receive him as our mighty Protector against the legions? "Today, if you hear his voice, do not harden your hearts" (Hebrews 4:7).

When the townspeople begged Jesus to leave them, he did. That is a judgment, isn't it? But Jesus did not just leave and judge. He had a follow-up plan. He did not give up so easily. He will not give up so easily on you and me.

## Study Questions

Couldn't Jesus have done more to keep the crowd from rejecting him? Or is that a bad question to ask? Explain.

Did Jesus care less about the townspeople than he did about the man who had been possessed? What in Mark's account leads you to your conclusion?

Look up Matthew 12:43-45. Evaluate how it was used in this chapter. Then write a short prayer based on Jesus' words in those verses.

Which of the four perspectives (Robert, Dawb, Jenny, or Jonathan) best fits the townspeople here? Explain your choice.

What needs to "begin today" for you?

Agree or disagree: I know when I am testing God's patience.

# CHAPTER
# FIVE

*"The man who had been demon-possessed begged to go with him." Mark 5:18*

"Sitting there, dressed and in his right mind" (Mark 5:15)—that is how Mark describes the man in the aftermath of the demons' departure into the pig herd. Luke adds that the man out of whom Jesus had cast the demons was "sitting at Jesus' feet" (8:35). It makes sense. After Jesus cleansed the man of demons, Jesus wanted to fill the man's heart and mind with good news, healing, bold faith, a new perspective for a new life. The posture of the man sitting at Jesus' feet probably communicates different things. In humility, the man showed his gratitude to Jesus by sitting at his feet. He was displaying honor to the one more powerful than demons, the Lord over heaven and earth and all that is in them. The man was worshiping Jesus. Certainly the man was listening to every single word that was coming out of the mouth of Jesus. Jesus had saved this man. It was completely understandable and perfectly appropriate for the man to beg, and to keep on begging, "Jesus, I want to stay with you!"

We have heard a lot of begging on this beach. The demons begged Jesus not to torture them. The demons begged Jesus not to drive them out of the area (Mark 5:10). The demons begged Jesus not to cast them into the Abyss (Luke 8:31). When the townspeople arrived to survey this scene, they did some begging too, asking Jesus please to go away. Of all the begging going on that day, the only begging that makes any sense at all was coming from this man who was sitting at Jesus' feet.

This man's life had been a nightmare of hopeless misery. One solitary demon living inside of him would have made his life a daily horror. But this man's bruised body had been host to a demon mob. From the first moment of his possession, there was no rest. But after Jesus had ordered the demons out, the man had rest. He had peace. He could begin his life again! How could we ever imagine the joy and relief of this man who was looking forward to his first night on a bed or any flat surface that did not bear the odor of decay? Even if he was too exhilarated to sleep that first night, he would not be driven into high mountain paths to wail and howl all night till dawn. And clean! He could be clean! Of course he begged to follow Jesus. He would serve Jesus willingly for life.

How would Jesus answer this grateful soul? He and the disciples were about to push off again for the Jewish side of the Sea of Galilee. A gentile travel companion would be difficult to explain, and the logistics would be quite challenging to manage. At this point in Jesus' ministry, though hardly exclusive to the Jewish people, he was still focused on his own people (Mark 7:27).

He would be in and out of a Jewish temple. Gentiles were not allowed to enter the temple of the Jews. A non-Jewish traveling disciple would not work.

The man would have to stay home. But would he have to stay silent?

Often, when on the Jewish side of the sea, Jesus required silence of those he rescued. Jesus did not want the people he healed and out of whom he drove demons to publish their good news. If the crowds grew too large too soon, this could force a response from Jesus' enemies before the appointed hour. Jesus had a time and a path. Nothing would take him off that path. Jesus in his time would announce, "The hour has come for the Son of Man to be glorified" (John 12:23). Also, though his efforts were in vain, Jesus wanted to limit the size of the crowds that gathered to lay their needs before him. Jesus wanted to teach and preach. Huge crowds made this difficult, near impossible. The more people Jesus rescued, the larger the crushing crowds that sought his help.

Would Jesus place those same restrictions upon this man, out of whom he had just evicted thousands of demons? The floodgates of hurting people would open if this man's story got out. This dramatic exorcism on the beach was a stunning display of power and compassion. Until the resurrection of Lazarus from four days in his tomb,[21] where in the Jewish community or any other community was there such a spectacle of Jesus' power over demons or disease or any human ill? If ever a recipient of Jesus' mercy should be discreet, it would be this man.

## Tell Your People

Although Jesus did not let the man become the 13th apostle, he gave him very important work to do: "Go home to your own people and tell them how much the Lord has done for you, and how he has had mercy on you" (Mark 5:19).

Jesus had no immediate plans for an extended teaching campaign in the Decapolis. He did not need, at this point, to concern himself with facing the demanding and cascading crowds there, surging and thundering for the Master's healing touch. He determined instead to send a missionary to them. Jesus commanded the man to serve his Lord and his God by telling everybody back at his home about the merciful acts of, to quote the demons, the Most High God.

Jesus had a high view of his new disciple. The man did not need more time to follow Jesus. He was now

---

[21] John 11:1-46

ready to proclaim the good news about Jesus. Whatever training was required for this glorious new position, for this status of being an ambassador and agent and herald of Jesus, took place in the time he sat at Jesus' feet. Then Jesus sent him.

The man once known as the demoniac had a new identity to share and a new story; it was his own. He experienced it. He was the one who was once possessed but who was then delivered. He started this day as he had started so many: dominated by demons. But before the end of this day, beneath the tombs that had been his home, he was delivered. A lot happened that day. Jesus saved a man and started a mission.

Jesus commissioned his forerunner to report what "the Lord" had done for him. If Jesus was referring to himself as the Lord, he had more than proved the integrity of his claim. But it does not seem to me that that would have been Jesus' style. Jesus' ministry on earth brought glory to his Father. Though Jesus probably did not call himself the Lord, the man whom he had delivered was happy and eager to do just that. Sent by Jesus to speak of the Lord's mercy, Mark's gospel reports that the man preached throughout the Decapolis everything that "Jesus had done for him" (5:20). Jesus' forerunner into the Decapolis amazed the residents with his testimony of the Lord's mercy. The testimony featured Jesus, the person who had driven out the demons. To this man, Jesus was the Lord. The Lord was Jesus. A sound conclusion, wouldn't you agree?

Jesus had directed the man to return to his "own people." The man's joy and gratitude and loyalty could not be so easily satisfied. The man who was once condemned to the solitary company of dead bones now roamed far and wide the streets of the living. Throughout the Decapolis, the man preached the deeds and mercy of Jesus. The word that Mark used to describe what this man was doing throughout the Decapolis is the same word that Mark used to describe what Jesus was doing from village to village (1:38) and what the disciples did from village to village (6:12): They were *preaching!*

Jesus did not despise this man's ethnic background or personal history. Life as a demon-possessed man who had spent time in ghastly tombs did not disqualify this man's mission as Jesus' forerunner into the Decapolis. Equipped and articulate with a heart full of gratitude, this man preached God's praises. Do you think he showed off, as an object lesson, his scars from those times the demons had him rip shackles off his wrists or made him cut himself with stones? Regardless, everyone who heard his preaching was amazed. The power of preaching was not and is not in the presenter or in the presenter's style or background. The amazing power of preaching is always in its main character, the Lord Jesus Christ, the Son of the Most High God, who commanded thousands of unclean spirits to depart from a man and to release their victim. And they did. And the man said, "Here I am to tell you what Jesus did, how he delivered me from a condition worse than death." And everyone was amazed.

## The Next Time

The next time Jesus came through the Decapolis, he was not anonymous. You should not be surprised. Jesus' advance publicist, the once-possessed man, had done his job. After the former demoniac had preached Jesus far and wide throughout the Decapolis, the townspeople no longer wanted Jesus to leave their area. They had been persuaded to ask Jesus to stick around, to heal, to help, and to save. The next time Mark's gospel takes his readers into the area of the Decapolis, we read of people bringing a deaf man for Jesus to heal. The townspeople "begged Jesus to place his hand on him" (Mark 7:32). Now that makes sense.

Begging Jesus to leave the Decapolis was a mistake. Begging Jesus to heal their hurting companion was a glorious act of faith.

On this trip through the Decapolis, Jesus commanded those whom he delivered to keep the good news of Jesus' kindness to themselves. Crowds of followers had become a problem also in the area of the Decapolis. Good job, ex-demoniac! The faithful work of this man whom Jesus had sent back to his own family produced for Jesus a new reputation in the region of the Decapolis.[22] The reputation of Jesus as the one who "has done everything well" (Mark 7:37) was spreading into new corners and among different peoples and tribes and families. The witness of the man who once slept in caves had amazed and astonished every audience. What a new life for this man! What a new work and purpose for his life! Jesus moved him from suffering in demonic darkness to spreading the gospel's light.

Jesus set out to save this man. It was on Jesus' list of things to do. Jesus traveled long roads and tolerated great trials also to rescue you. Just after Jesus rescued Zacchaeus from the darkness he was living in, Jesus announced his holy purpose: "The Son of Man came

---

[22] The Bible does not directly attribute the Decapolis region's subsequent interest in Jesus to the demoniac's testimony. I believe it is a legitimate deduction based on Mark 5:20.

to seek and to save the lost" (Luke 19:10). Jesus sought you out and then saved you. What a splendid thought! What did Jesus' journey require? The journey to rescue you was brutal as Jesus walked through the injustice of his religious community's court system and then through the brutality of the Roman judicial system. But not until Jesus reached a hill outside of Jerusalem did he endure the deepest wounds. Jesus carried his own cross, with the help of Simon of Cyrene, to that hill. It is still there. The hill is called Golgotha. Three crosses jutted out from its crest when Jesus was lifted up on his. Jesus was nailed to the cross in the middle. The pain Jesus endured there was the full penalty for every human's sin. The Father required this payment from his Son. His Son was willing. "Yet not what I will, but what you will," Jesus said (Mark 14:36).

That blood of Jesus, the innocent Lamb of God, purchased freedom for the world and for you. As others have said, it was not nails that held Jesus to that cross. It was his will and his Father's will to save all people. What looked to the world like utter failure was in fact the great victory of God over Satan and his demons. The accuser could no longer accuse. Jesus had borne the burden of every sin Satan could charge us with. There is no shame. Jesus endured it. There will be no punishment. Jesus suffered it. Satan's power has been crushed. You belong to God now. You are his prized possession. You are his. He is yours.

### The Joy of Being Rescued

Jesus is still rescuing people from demon possession. Jesus is still rescuing people from Satan's hidden attacks on human hearts, in which he wants to curse and shame and humiliate. And when weak and trembling humans are delivered by this powerful yet tender Lord, there is joy.

If a newspaper reporter from the *Decapolis Daily News* wanted to do a story for the community on the man whom Jesus rescued from thousands of demons, one of the first questions the reporter would ask would be, "How did you feel in that moment when all the demons left your body?" I would enjoy hearing the man's reply to that question. How did it feel to be possessed? How did it feel to be saved from all of those demons? I would like to hear the man express the full range of his emotions in that one day when he went from plagued lunatic to calm follower of Jesus—in his right mind, fully dressed, and sitting at the feet of his Lord. What did that feel like?

We can try to imagine how this man Jesus healed might express his many emotions. But we cannot know what he felt two millennia ago. We do know what emotions people experience who have been rescued in our day. "Elizabeth" would love to have you know her story. A pastor and some of his fellow Christians from a Southeast Asia immigrant community came to visit her in her Midwest American home. The family of Elizabeth had invited this pastor to come and pray for her because evil spirits were causing her and her family tremendous suffering.

Elizabeth's situation was extremely difficult. The process that this pastor and his members went through before the demon finally left was long and agonizing. But the power of Jesus and the power of the prayers from the people of Jesus prevailed. Finally, Elizabeth was free of the evil spirit inside of her. What did Elizabeth say? How did she feel when the demon departed? She said, "I am really happy. I know the demon is gone. What was controlling me is no longer in me. I feel clean. I am who I am now. I no longer feel controlled. I feel happy."

The pastor who provided this wonderful ministry also felt joy. All that he and his people suffered in order to pray this demon out of Elizabeth bore the fruit of freedom. Elizabeth was free. The pastor witnessed the great joy of Elizabeth. He and his prayer team shared the joy of Elizabeth. Jesus is the powerful one. He is more powerful than demons.

This same pastor has shared with me that people rescued from demons become wonderful church members. This pastor's goal is not merely wonderful church members. His goal, of course, is to help people out of great misery through prayer and preaching Jesus' good news. But those whom he has escorted out of demons' clutches do make great church members. A pastor appreciates great church members. The rescued believers work hard to strengthen the ministry that rescued them and to participate as they can in all that the congregation does for its members and community. Their joyful witness amazes and inspires both the church members and their community.

## Cleansed Twice-Over

After Elizabeth's incredible rescue from the trauma of demons inside of her, do you think she might have feared their return? God forbid that this little girl should harbor such a dread! What could her pastor do to protect her and to encourage her? What he could do—what he *did* do—was baptize her. Elizabeth was rescued. Then she was instructed. And, finally, she was baptized. Elizabeth's rescue from demons was incredible. What happened at her baptism, what she received at her baptism, is even more incredible! Hard to believe? Read on!

Remember after her rescue, when Elizabeth said that she felt clean? In her baptism, Elizabeth was cleansed again. Notice how clean baptism's "washing with water through the word" makes us according to the apostle Paul:

> Christ loved the church and gave himself up for her to make her holy, cleansing her by the washing with water through the word, and to present her to himself as a radiant church, without stain or wrinkle or any other blemish, but holy and blameless.[23]

Here God promises us a washing in Baptism that removes every stain of sin, every wrinkle, blame, and blemish that might show how very long we have lived by the guidance of unclean spirits. The same powerful Word that drives out hell's legions gave power to the plain water poured over Elizabeth's head. It made her ready for Jesus Christ, ready to be presented to him radiant and holy.

After her rescue from demons, Elizabeth said she felt free from the demon's control; she was restored

---

[23] Ephesians 5:25-27

to herself. She said, "I am who I am now." With her identity restored and the tyrants evicted, doors opened for Elizabeth. Chains fell off. She transitioned from victim to victor. Quite a journey, yes? But at her baptism, she got more! Again, the apostle Paul says, "Now it is God who makes both us and you stand firm in Christ. He anointed us, set his seal of ownership on us, and put his Spirit in our hearts as a deposit, guaranteeing what is to come."[24] The "anointing" that sealed God's ownership of Elizabeth was her baptism. It's a good thing to be "owned" by God. He takes care of what is his. He deposits his Holy Spirit into his children as a down payment and guarantee of all that they will receive when they join him in heaven. God's seal—Baptism—is like a blazing shield that declares to Satan and his demons, "Here Is God's Possession. Hands Off!" How is that for an open door, freedom, identity, strength, and victory?

Finally, what Elizabeth and all those who love her wanted to know was that Satan's demons could not come back. These people wanted rest from the ordeal they had been through; they wanted the assurance that these demons had been driven out and defeated to the point that they could not come back. Elizabeth

---

[24] 2 Corinthians 1:21,22

received this assurance when she was baptized. Reflect on the following words that our friend Paul wrote to the Colossians—he packs so many beautiful thoughts into these sentences,[25] but I will emphasize the parts that talk about Baptism and the defeat and disarming of Satan's demons:

In Christ all the fullness of the Deity lives in bodily form, and *in Christ you have been brought to fullness.* He is the head over every power and authority. In him you were also circumcised with a circumcision not performed by human hands. Your whole self ruled by the flesh was put off when you were circumcised by Christ, *having been buried with him in baptism, in which you were also raised with him* through your faith in the working of God, who raised him from the dead.

When you were dead in your sins and in the uncircumcision of your flesh, *God made you alive with Christ.* He forgave us all our sins, having canceled the charge of our legal indebtedness, which stood

---

[25] The first sentence in the following quote is an especially important Bible verse. It is one of Saint Paul's most explicit explanations of who and what Jesus is: Jesus is truly human, but not just human. He is also true God. There is not any way in which he is not God's equal. The new "circumcision" of which Paul speaks further on in the quote is Baptism. As circumcision was important to God's Old Testament people as a seal of their relationship with God, so now Baptism is a precious sign and seal for us New Testament followers of Jesus.

against us and condemned us; he has taken it away, nailing it to the cross. *And having disarmed the powers and authorities, he made a public spectacle of them, triumphing over them by the cross.*[26]

Paul explains who and what we are: We are alive in Jesus, forgiven by Jesus, filled up completely with Jesus, buried with Jesus, and raised to a new spiritual life of faith and trust in Jesus. When Elizabeth was baptized, she was filled with the Lord Jesus, who disarmed Satan's authority and the demons' power. Jesus not only disarmed them, he so completely triumphed over them by his cross that these dreadful demons were humiliated. Jesus "filled" Elizabeth with every glorious gift of grace that she would ever need to stand firm against every attack of the evil one. Baptism filled Elizabeth with the fullness of Jesus. The powerful and loving Savior took over as the authority and ruler in her heart.

Clearly my goal in these paragraphs is not only to celebrate what Jesus gave to Elizabeth in her baptism. I am talking to you. You must be convinced that this same sure sign and perfect seal of your complete victory over Satan is in your possession even now. When

[26] Colossians 2:9–15

you were baptized—or when you will be baptized—you were given God's guarantee that you will stand against Satan and live with God in his heaven. Through Baptism, God shares with you his Son's complete victory over the devil and every one of his demons.[27]

Now connect all of this back to that beach with Jesus and the healed man. Do you remember the man sitting calmly at Jesus' feet, enjoying and displaying the fact that he was in his right mind? Filled with joy, free from the control of thousands of demons, in possession of himself, now a possession of his dear Savior, he begged Jesus to allow him to follow after Jesus; he wanted to remain with Jesus. But Jesus said, "Actually, I need you to go back to your people to tell them what God has done for you." Jesus now sends us. He says, "Go. . . . I am with you always" (Matthew 28:19,20). He says, "Peace be with you! As the Father has sent me, I am sending you" (John 20:21). We are rescued. Let us now go rescue.

---

[27] A believer can give up the blessings received in Baptism by turning away in unbelief. But neither Satan nor his demons could ever take over or destroy the immortal soul of the believer who has received the seal of Baptism. Jesus says in John 10:27-29, "My sheep listen to my voice; I know them, and they follow me. I give them eternal life, and they will never perish; no one will snatch them out of my hand. My Father, who has given them to me, is greater than all; no one can snatch them out of my Father's hand."

## A Perspective: Joyful Confidence
## That I Am Safe With Jesus

The best perspective on demons is to consider them—to see them—in their completely defeated state. The Bible's poetry soars when it proclaims Jesus' victory over the devil, death, and the grave. Just one example of such a hymn of glory is in Romans, where the apostle Paul says,

Who shall separate us from the love of Christ? Shall trouble or hardship or persecution or famine or nakedness or danger or sword? No, in all these things we are more than conquerors through him who loved us. For I am convinced that neither death nor life, neither angels nor demons, neither the present nor the future, nor any powers, neither height nor depth, nor anything else in all creation, will be able to separate us from the love of God that is in Christ Jesus our Lord. (Romans 8:35,37-39)

That says it. That is the best perspective. There is no better perspective than complete and overwhelming victory. That victory is ours in Jesus. We have not been destroyed by demons, nor shall we be. We are safe in Jesus' family where no power can harm us. Our perspective says, "Stay near this one!" Get close to Jesus. Closer still! We get closer through our daily

Bible reading. So read! We get closer through our regular prayers for ourselves and for all of God's children. Our perspective, and the best perspective nurtured by our reading, finds us close to our Savior, continually praying to him and praising him! We pray for constant protection from every attack of the devil. We praise Jesus for his faithful protection in this life and even in death. This is where we want to be. This is where we want our family and friends to be.

Ah, but what if my rescue hasn't come yet? What if I am still suffering because of some demons, still crying out over some uncleanness they have me stuck in? Can I still have this joyful perspective of victory?

## Study Questions

Reread Elizabeth's story. How does her story affect you? Does it add something significant to your perspective on demons?

What are some things you do to stay close to Jesus? some things you need to start doing? How will you go about this? What could you do to help yourself follow through on your new commitments?

People will wear a cross to remind them of their Savior's love and help. In what ways is our baptism into Jesus and into the Christian faith much more than a reminder?

An author recently wrote to his fellow Christians, "The world has certainly rarely thought of us as 'joy experts.'"[28] Do you agree? Give a few reasons for your answer. Does this chapter provide any kind of solution to the problem that this quote presents? If so, what?

Do you think the man understood why Jesus wouldn't let him come along? How did he demonstrate that he did not hold a grudge against Jesus for sending him back home?

---

[28] Prof. Jeffrey A. Ochswald, "Faithful Witness in Suffering and Joy," *Concordia Journal,* Vol. 41, No. 2 (Spring 2015), p. 125.

How would it show in your life if you had a perspective of complete victory over the demons?

The chapter imagined a reporter from the *Decapolis Daily News* interviewing the man who had been freed from Legion. Write what you think a part of that interview might have looked like.

Look up the story of Zacchaeus in Luke chapter 19. Why did that story come up here? Find several similarities between Jesus' dealings with Zacchaeus and his dealings with the demoniac in our story.

# CHAPTER
# SIX

*"Jesus was in the stern, sleeping
on a cushion. The disciples woke
him and said to him, 'Teacher,
don't you care if we drown?'"*
*Mark 4:38*

How long had the demon-possessed man been demon-possessed before Jesus stepped onto that shore? We are not told. How many times had the demon-possessed man lifted up his eyes to the sky and cried out, "If there is a god up there, help me"? We can only imagine. How many times had people tried to restrain this man only to have chains and irons smashed against the caves? No matter how long this man had struggled with thousands of demons, it no doubt felt like it was far too long.

Pain makes time stop. Seconds become minutes and hours when we are in a lot of pain. Pain hurts, but it also has a way to make us feel alone. Pain makes us feel afraid. It is that way for me anyway. Has anyone ever told you that you do not handle pain well? My response is, "It has never been my goal to handle pain. I prefer to get rid of it!" Though you might express yourself with more poise, wouldn't you agree? We do not want to experience suffering. We do not want to learn how to suffer. When we are suffering, we are impatient for physical and emotional relief from pain.

Christians suffer all kinds of pain. There is the every-day kind of pain. Christians get sick and incur injuries. There is also the pain that God sends Christians to help them grow in their faith and service. Jesus has warned us that his Father might prune back even the branches that are already bearing fruit so that they will bear more fruit (John 15:2). The pruning that the Father does to us hurts. We understand that this Fatherly pruning makes us more fruitful . . . but it hurts! Christians also suffer the pain of persecution. The devil and this world hated Jesus. They hate us who follow Jesus as well. Jesus gives us promises of persecutions, along with the words to say to those who persecute us.[29] Christians all over the world suffer intense persecutions even to the point of death.

## Mental Illness, Physical Illness, and Demons

But how much of the pain we suffer is caused by demons?

Our skeptic friend would insist that illness must be explained, diagnosed, and treated in a physical way. Mental illness and depression, for example, are the result of a chemical or hormonal imbalance. Physical illness comes from germs, environmental factors, or genetics. Emotional pain comes out of unhealthy mental self-messaging, unreasonable expectations, or counterproductive subconscious desires. Addiction is

[29] Luke 12:11

a sickness that can be predicted in people with genetic predispositions—addiction is physical. "Demons do not make us sick!" Our skeptical friend, Robert, will not allow us to suggest that demons are in any way responsible for our physical maladies. And part of me too is saying, "Don't blame demons for suicidal thoughts."

There are in the Bible, however, many examples of physical and emotional troubles brought on by the devil and demons. Luke tells the story of an evil spirit that had crippled a woman for 18 years (13:11). Paul pleaded with the Lord three times to remove from him a painful "thorn," a health trouble of some kind (2 Corinthians 12:7). God told Paul that he was going to keep him weak with this thorn so he could remain strong in his Lord. God gave the devil permission to bring all manner of suffering upon Job. Satan's purpose was to destroy Job by taking away his wealth, his children, his reputation, his physical health, and also most certainly his spiritual and emotional strength. God allowed Satan to do this to test Job. Job knew what was going on. In the depth of his bodily and emotional pain, he cried out in faith, "[The LORD] knows the way that I take; when he has tested me, I will come forth as gold" (Job 23:10).

Certainly I am not saying that all depression can be attributed to Satan. But it is an equally misguided oversimplification to say that Satan never causes depression. And Satan can lead a Christian to commit suicide. In my ministry as a pastor, I have conducted Christian funeral services for sincere Christians who did—in a moment of weakness, in a moment of severe Satanic testing—bring death upon themselves. But in my ministry to these people, I knew the depth of their faith as well as the depth of their struggle. I have no doubt that Satan was working hard to do what he loves to do: destroy humans.

The Bible reports that Satan was involved in the physical and mental and spiritual suffering of people in Bible days. Why would we think that Satan is not still trying to afflict Christians in this way today? I am not saying that all mental illness and depression is brought on by demons. Expert health care professionals and amazing medicines are esteemed agents of God's healing touch. But to insist that the devil and his demons are never involved in the inner struggles of God's people—all people—is not the best perspective.

Why? If we deny that our various pains and heartaches and emotional struggles come from demons, we are thereby denying ourselves tremendous opportunities for comfort and healing. If these things are coming from Satan, let us not hesitate to ask our powerful Lord Jesus to rescue us from Satan! And if God is allowing Satan to bring these troubles to us, as he did with Job, let us not hesitate to pray to God to accomplish quickly the purpose for which he has sent to us this test. God only disciplines those he loves (Proverbs 3:12). God only disciplines those he accepts as his children (Hebrews 12:6). Somehow, even the things that hurt me can be a blessing to me and can help me grow (John 15:2).

## Be Patient; Do Not Fear

Christians are called upon to learn how to handle pain, including pain brought on by demons. As we work together to develop a good perspective about demons, I propose that fearless patience has a place in this perspective.

Just before the exorcism of Legion that we have been studying, the disciples of Jesus got their perspectives challenged in a dramatic way.

They and Jesus had spent the entire day on the shore of the Sea of Galilee opposite from where the demon-possessed lived. After hours spent teaching the thronging Jewish crowds, Jesus directed the disciples to give him a break from those throngs and sail him across to the gentile shore. Jesus was in charge. Jesus set the schedule for the day. But Mark says that the disciples "took [Jesus] along, just as he was, in the boat" (4:36). Does that phrase suggest a shift in authority? Could it be that at least the first four disciples—Peter, Andrew, James, and John, who were experienced sailors—felt that they should be in charge, at least now while they were in a boat upon the sea? These men had been career fishermen. The boat was their area of expertise. The water was their second home. Jesus? He was a teacher, and before that, a carpenter. What did he know about boats and winds and points of sail?

Maybe Mark's language hints not only at the boat-handling expertise of some of the disciples but also at the complete unpreparedness of Jesus when he entered the boat. Jesus entered the boat "just as he was." So Jesus did not have sailing gear. He did not participate in the prelaunch checklist. He did not plan ahead to have with him the kind of clothes that "real" sailors might have liked to wear on sea crossings. Mark, a superb storyteller, is setting the stage for us with the phrase "just as he was."

Jesus did not care about who had the authority or how efficiently the ship was steered. He was exhausted. He made for the soft cushions in the rear of the boat—the stern, a sailor would say—and fell asleep. Jesus slipped into a very deep sleep.

It is interesting to see how the gospels of Matthew, Mark, and Luke report the storm that suddenly overtook this boat on the Sea of Galilee. Matthew describes the storm with a word usually translated "earthquake." And it was a "furious" earthquake of a storm (8:24). Luke reports that a "hurricane of wind" came down upon the sea (8:23). Mark too wants his readers to know that it was a "furious" hurricane of wind that came down on the sea (4:37). Waves were breaking over the boat and filling it up! As experienced as some of these sailors were, they had not experienced a storm like this. The boat was no longer their boat. The sea was no longer their sea. Like helpless children, they fell upon the sleeping teacher: "Don't you care if we drown?" "Save us!" "We are going to die!"

Whatever sailor bravado was on the boat before the storm got washed overboard with the disciples' gear. Now they feared for their lives. They were confused by their teacher's calm. Jesus could sleep through a hurricane on the open sea! Mark tells us that they did not know what kind of man this Jesus was. But they knew that they should wake him up before the boat sank and the sailors drowned.

Jesus woke up. He stood up. He rebuked the wind and the waves: "Quiet! Be still!" And there was an immediate calm. This sudden calm had to have been as unsettling as the terrible storm. Jesus turned to his wide-eyed disciples. He rebuked them as harshly as he did the storm: "Why are you so afraid? Do you still have no faith?" That truly is an interesting question. How was it possible that the disciples still apparently had no faith? Already at this point in their career as intern apostles, they had watched Jesus heal the crowds of their sicknesses and diseases. The disciples had watched Jesus make leprous skin whole and the paralyzed dance for joy. They had heard amazing sermons daily. Although his biggest exorcism, as we have heard, would be later that evening, they had already watched Jesus drive out demons with a word. Maybe now they noticed that Jesus had used the same word to silence demons that he just used to silence the storm! But what they had noticed most recently was that he was sleeping through a terrible storm. How could Jesus be upset at the disciples for shaking him awake in their panic? "Why are you so afraid?" Who would not be afraid?

## A Perspective: The Lord Never Sleeps

Remember that this miracle and this rebuke happened just before they all met Legion. How is it all connected?

Imagine for a moment that the disciples did not panic. A terrible storm did not upset the disciples. They let the teacher sleep. What perspective would have allowed them to do that and so to avoid a scolding from Jesus for being afraid? What would the disciples have had to keep in mind to convince themselves, despite the shearing winds and the inches of water pooling up ankle-deep in the boat, that they really weren't about to drown?

That perspective, that kind of nearly unimaginable confidence, sounds like this: "Awake or asleep, Jesus will guard my life, attend to my needs, and take care of me.[30] Bad storm or not, pain and distress or not, Jesus is still right here."

---

[30] Jesus was sleeping physically according to the needs of his human nature, but he would never fall asleep on any of his children in terms of his divine care.

Jesus must have thought that this was a possible perspective or even the assumed perspective. Why else would he have been disappointed in the disciples for being afraid during the storm?

Maybe the disciples were confused. They could have quoted to one another verses from Psalm 121, a familiar psalm that promises God's protection. The psalm says,

*"Your Protector will not slumber. Indeed, the Protector of Israel does not slumber or sleep." (verses 3b,4 HCSB)*

There is a great promise. But their Protector was sleeping! They could see him, soaking wet but eyes closed—oblivious. What do you do when the sky is falling and your Protector is taking a nap? Trust that the promise hasn't been canceled.

Isn't the lesson the same when we face a storm of fallen angels instead of falling rain and lightning?

Look at a few verses of Psalm 44.

*"Wake up, LORD! Why are You sleeping? Get up! Don't reject us forever!" (verse 23 HCSB)*

In Psalm 44, the psalmist reveals his frustration and confusion. On one hand, he knows the truth and has experienced the truth that God is his Protector, a reliable Warrior King, by whose strength he can stand against any foe. On the other hand, in spite of what he knows in his heart, his eyes see a different reality. The psalmist sees his enemies dominating, mocking, ridiculing, and winning. When it appears that arrogant enemies are conquering, continuing in a quiet faith seems very difficult. The psalmist cries out, "Wake up, LORD!" The disciples cried out, "Wake up, Teacher!"

The Bible lets us listen in on these prayers prayed by believers in times of doubts and fears. But this is not to justify our doubts and fears. It is to show us that, at the end of the day, there is in fact no reason for doubts and fears. Especially when we are afraid, God invites us to pray,

> *"Rise up! Help us! Redeem us because of Your faithful love." (verse 26 HCSB)*

We have very dangerous enemies. They are far more powerful and cunning than the human enemies the psalmist was facing. Our strength won't be enough. Our enemies seem to attack most fiercely when our defenses are down. When we are tired or sick, when stress is making us feel alone, or when pain is making us feel fear, that is when the devil attacks our hearts with his ancient lies: "Where is your God now?" "God is sleeping! You are on your own!"

Or sometimes these unclean enemies settle in for a long siege. Their goal: to wear us down over the long haul. The longer we suffer their spiritual, mental, or even physical attacks and the longer it seems to take to get an answer to our prayers, the more obvious it seems to be that the Savior's eyes must be closed tight, oblivious.

When we are in pain, chronic or sudden, we can be impatient. When we are suffering, we may feel afraid. It is confusing. "But he knows the way that I take; when he has tested me, I will come forth as gold" (Job 23:10). As I wait to be delivered, I wait to come forth as gold. As I wait for my family members or friends to be delivered, I wait for them to come forth as gold. We will be tested with fire but not consumed. Rather, we will be purified like gold, pruned to be more fruitful even though we are now fruitful, having everything—even with persecutions. With God's strength made perfect in our weakness, we know that whether awake or asleep, the Lord watches over us. This is a really good perspective. This is the best one. The truth is that God will deliver you and me in his time, at just the right time, because of his faithful love.

Jesus assures us, "Do not be afraid, little flock, for your Father has been pleased to give you the kingdom" (Luke 12:32).

## Study Questions

Agree or disagree: My medications will work more effectively if, while I'm taking them, I pray for help against demons.

How does the story of the calming of the storm prepare the reader of Mark's gospel for the story of Jesus driving out Legion?

What can you do now to prepare for the next time demons are allowed to bring affliction into your life?

Do you see a difference between the statements "God allowed Satan to afflict me" and "God sent affliction to me"?

Would it be better to go to a doctor who believes demons bear some responsibility for illnesses than to a doctor who denies this altogether?

Evaluate: "If I blame demons for the painful or difficult episodes in my life, my friends will think I've lost my mind."

Do you have pain in your life right now? Does someone close to you? Describe how this chapter might help with handling that pain.

Have you ever thought God has gone to sleep on you? Explain.

# CHAPTER
# SEVEN

*"If it is by the Spirit of God
that I drive out demons, then
the kingdom of God has come
upon you." Matthew 12:28*

If we back up even further on this amazing day in Jesus' ministry, we can add one more important ingredient to our perspective on the demon world. As we have heard, Jesus began this day on the opposite shore of this sea, spending hours teaching the Jewish crowds.

The seashore offered a nice open space. The surface of the water would help the sound of a voice to travel. Jesus got into a boat and pushed out a little ways from the beach to make it easier to preach to such a large crowd.

Then Jesus told stories, parables. In the first parable, Jesus talked about the different places seeds landed after a farmer tossed those seeds into his field. Some of the seed did not make it into the good dirt of the farmer's field. Some seed landed on the hard path around the field. The birds would descend upon that seed on the path and eat it up.

Later on that day, Jesus' disciples asked him to explain that first parable. Regarding the seed that fell on the path, Jesus explained, "Some people are like seed along the path, where the word is sown. As soon as they hear it, Satan comes and takes away the word that was sown in them" (Mark 4:15). Notice: This parable had evil angels in it. They were the seed-snatching birds, and the seed they snatched was God's Word, the news of the Savior.

I'm sure the disciples felt very different hearing a parable with demons in it under the morning seashore sunlight than they felt hours later when the sun had gone down and they were hearing the actual voices of thousands of these demons shrieking out Jesus' name. Demons turning a man into a violent, flesh-rending monster seems much more dreadful than demons snatching sermons out of people's ears. But they are all the same demons, aren't they? With the same unclean hatred. Jesus wants us to understand that we will meet more of these demons every time we hear the Word of Jesus. Every time a person hears the Word, Satan's henchmen want to snatch it away.

I wonder if this is especially true for people who are hearing God's Word for the first time. As a pastor of a congregation, I had many opportunities to share the good news of Jesus with people who had never heard it. It was exciting to watch people begin to understand that Jesus saved them from a burdened conscience and from eternal punishment through his innocent sufferings on the cross. The joy and peace that Jesus' gospel planted in the hearts of these people blossomed! But as joy increased, so did the attacks of Satan. It was obvious in so many situations that the devil was doing everything in his power to drag these new Christians back into his congregation of the dead. Temptations increased. Troubles arose. Old problems flared up.

"Terry" was one of these new Christians whom the devil unwillingly released to the kingdom of Christ. Because Terry had enrolled his children in our congregation's Lutheran elementary school, he took our Bible information course for new Christians. He took that course three times actually. Every time he enrolled one of his children in our school, I asked him to take this course on the basic teachings of the Bible. He did. But throughout each course, all he did was argue, deny, and scoff. I took Terry through the course privately each time so that he would not frustrate other people taking the course with his constant challenges and arguments.

Out of the blue—15 years after our last meeting—he called to tell me that he wanted me to be his pastor. I was incredulous at first. It was just too dramatic of a turnaround to accept. But we started the Bible information class again for the fourth time. And this time, Terry received every doctrine and promise from the pages of Scripture as pure gold and indisputable truth. Terry's studies in the Bible proceeded wonderfully. His personal life, however, took a definite downward turn. Coinciding perfectly with his new faith in Jesus, Terry's wife left him, lifelong friends betrayed him, one of his children refused to be reconciled with him, he lost financial security, and he became very ill. I think the devil thought that he had Terry. As we discussed all of his new trials and troubles, it seemed to Terry that Satan was particularly angry at him for leaving unbelief behind.

Terry received a Christian funeral less than a year after he stood up in front of our church—as all new members did—to give a public confession of faith in Jesus. Terry had received the seal and assurance of his victory over Satan by being baptized. He had been strengthened in that victory through the many times he received Holy Communion with his family of believers. Then he died. But he died with thanksgiving and praise on his lips . . . and with a regret. He regretted that he had not started his Christian journey with Jesus earlier in his life, much earlier. But Terry died free and victorious in Jesus.

Satan does not need to "possess" a person who does not believe in Jesus. Satan does not need to send demons into that person's body, because he already is in possession of the soul. But when the gospel is preached, Satan risks losing his control. He will not let this happen without giving his best efforts to gobble up the seed cast upon that path, to snatch away the Word that was preached to that person.

We need to add this to our perspective on demons. Satan hates what you and I are doing right now: trying to learn about Jesus. He hates you. He wants to destroy you. So he will do everything he can to take this message away from you. And perhaps, if you are new to the Christian faith or considering a return to the Christian faith, Satan may unleash bold attacks against this Word so that you stop thinking about a new perspective on demons altogether. Even if you are a lifelong Christian, Satan does not want you to freshen up your perspective regarding him. If you are a religious professional like me, Satan will try to complicate your schedule so that he can wolf down this Word. Satan surely does not want to see a stronger witness against him and for Jesus! Whoever you are and wherever you are when you hear the Word of God, the good news of Jesus, Satan will want to remove that Word before it can take root in your heart and bear fruit for the harvest.

I wonder how many times Satan ruined a Sunday afternoon in my home. I would study God's Word to prepare a sermon for my congregation. I would preach that sermon to my congregation. I was built up by the Word. I was built up because I enjoyed the privilege of sharing that Word with God's people. I was enjoying joy and peace in abundance. I was happy.

Then I would go home and instigate a silly squabble with my wife or with one of my children. Peace gone. Joy disappeared.

Satan saw seed on the path. The Word had been sown, but it did not remain in my heart. Satan snatched it up. I was too immature to see what was happening. It was completely my fault. I do not blame anyone else, including Satan. I let it happen. Maybe it happened because Satan surprised me. Maybe I proudly assumed such hostility could not rise up in my Christian home. I do not know how it happened or maybe even why. I do know that Satan saw seed on the path. Those times when a beautiful Sunday was spoiled by conflict, the seed had fallen on a hard path instead of good dirt.

### Their Most Fearsome Tactic

Until you "see" the ways evil spirits try to take God's Word away from us, you have not yet seen Satan at his best ... or worst. We have looked at many ways demons attack us. They want to make us suffer, to give us pain, to fill us with fear, to enslave us, to make us filthy in every way they can. But what is the demons' main goal, their keenest desire? However wide their trail of destruction, however bitter the suffering they cause, and however deep the wounds, demons are not and cannot be satisfied until they take us away from our God.

We may be distracted from this overarching strategy of the demons, but they never are. When we even take the time to think about demons, we may find most disturbing the potential of their open attacks on our mental and physical health, or their dramatic horror-movie-style assaults that put the power of the occult on bold display.

But there is a method of demonic attack that we should consider much more disturbing. The demons may tie it to some brash and ugly show of their power. Or they may bring it to your heart discreetly, leaving faint footprints.

What is the devil's favorite and most fearsome way to hurt humans? He lies. He knows that when we still have God's truth in our hearts, we still have God. So when humans already have God's truth, the devil wants to put his lies in its place. Deceit is his favorite tactic. It is his favorite language. When the devil lies, he is speaking his "native language" (John 8:44). In other words, lying is easy for him and he is good at it.

It is easy to see how terrible the devil's lies are by recalling one of his very first lies. God said, "You must not eat from the tree of the knowledge of good and evil, for when you eat from it you will certainly die" (Genesis 2:17). But the devil invited Eve to eat this fruit and promised her that she would certainly not die. The devil, clothed in a serpent's scales, came to Eve and said, "You will not certainly die" (Genesis 3:4). Then the devil told another lie: "God knows that when you eat from it your eyes will be opened, and you will be like God, knowing good and evil" (Genesis 3:5).

This lie was as external, confrontational, face-to-face, and obvious as any attack could be. The devil was saying, "Stop being so naïve: the sooner you stop listening to God, the sooner you can really start living! God doesn't love you as much as you think." Because Adam and Eve bought this lie, sin and death came into this world. Because of this sin, Satan gained access to us in this world. And, more to the point, we became susceptible to Satan's favorite form of attacking humans in this world: his lies.

And here's his favorite lie: "God doesn't love you as much as you think." All the hosts of hell are well trained. They know they must destroy our confidence in God's love if they are to take us away from him.

Pains and external assaults give the demons ample opportunity to try to put that lie into your heart and mind. But Satan has discreet approaches too.

We have a pretty clear idea as to what kind of people we want to be. Most of us would like to be and be regarded as good people. We do not begin our adult lives with a wish to bring shame on our name, to commit the kinds of crimes that would separate us from our community, to alienate our closest kin, or to betray and backstab dear friends. We do not set out to do any of that.

Then, the thought occurs to us, "What has being good ever gotten me?" One day, we say to ourselves, "No one will know." Frustrated, we conclude, "I deserve this one little fling, this episode of raw adventure." When we cannot stand the voice anymore, we submit, because "Why should I be the only one on this lonely high road?" We did not set out to fail, to compromise everything we stand for. But we did.

A person should get another chance. We should be able to pick up the pieces and just move on. But it rarely works that way, right? The devil and how many thousands of demons managed to persuade us to do this wrong thing this one time. He gave us a dozen good lies, each of which at the time made a ton of sense. And if we could just move on after falling to his lies, we might escape things like shame or consequences or punishment . . . or failure. But the devil and his demons are not done with us, not yet. After they trick us with reasonable lies, they begin a torment that makes us long for the lonely tombs of the Decapolis. The voice that once charmed us now haunts us. Once alluring, now screeching, the devil stirs up our consciences to ask, "What is this terrible thing you have done? How could you have done this? What were you thinking? You fool! You failure! You have really thrown away God's love this time!"

The demoniac carved designs into his uncovered flesh and walked dark mountain paths at night, howling. Awful. But if the demons would have broken his teeth and crushed his bones, that pain would not have compared to that of his broken spirit, guilty conscience, and despairing fearful heart. I know how long it takes me to heal from a broken bone. I am still waiting for my crushed ego, my broken heart, my betrayed dreams to heal. When will I forget the sins of my youth? When can I move on after that one small compromise that one single time? The terrible truth is, Satan—and that name of his means "accuser"—will till my last day accuse me and shame me for the very crimes he tricked me into committing.

I said above that Satan's soldiers know how to leave *faint* footprints when they need to. Hidden and secret enemies, they speak lies to the heart. We do what we do not want to do and what we would never imagine that we could do. And having done it, the devil humiliates us with a cruel effect. He rips us to shreds. He tells us we have stepped outside of God's love. We cannot bear Satan's mocking and his condemning. Sleep? Not much. Moving on? Not far.

These are not original thoughts. The psalms show the depth of pain caused by a troubled conscience. David grieves in Psalm 38, "My wounds fester and are loathsome because of my sinful folly. I am bowed down and brought very low; all day long I go about mourning. I am feeble and utterly crushed; I groan in anguish of heart" (verses 5,6,8).

Martin Luther spoke clearly about these attacks of conscience in which Satan would condemn and shame. His words reveal not only his personal experience with the devil's attacks but the depth of pain these attacks effected. Even a hero of faith like him can say:

Then comes the devil, who baits and badgers us on all sides, but especially exerts himself where the conscience and spiritual matters are concerned. His purpose is to . . . drive us into despair, denial of

God, blasphemy, and countless other abominable sins.[31] . . . He crushes some and drives others to insanity; some he drowns in water, and many he hounds to suicide or other dreadful catastrophes. Therefore, there is nothing for us to do on earth but to pray without ceasing against this archenemy. For if God did not support us, we would not be safe from him for a single hour.[32]

A good perspective on the devil and demons is to recognize the terrible lies they place upon our hearts. Satan is lying when he tells us that God's ways rob of us life and adventure. And when we do fall to these lies, as we are often inclined to do, Satan is lying when he tells us that there is no hope for us and that God does not love us. These attacks hurt the worst. They reveal the devil at his "best." They reveal just how unclean this head demon is, and every other demon who is with him in the Abyss.

I have made it easy for these enemies to attack me from the outside and from the inside. I cope with my shame—not well—instead of dealing with it as God

---

[31] The Large Catechism, The Lord's Prayer, *The Book of Concord: The Confessions of the Evangelical Lutheran Church*, edited by Robert Kolb and Timothy J. Wengert (Minneapolis: Augsburg Fortress Press, 2000), p. 454.

[32] The Large Catechism, The Lord's Prayer, Kolb-Wengert, pp. 455-456.

invites his children to deal with it: by reflecting on his promises to me in his Word and in my baptism and by receiving strength and forgiveness through his Holy Supper. Bad coping makes me bad company. It helps little to say to people around me that I am unfriendly because I do not like myself.

### "The Kingdom of God Has Come Upon You!"

If Satan's most favorite tactic, his most cherished lie, is to tell you that you have done too much wrong to be forgiven, that someone like you ought to feel crushed and hopeless and ought to be tormented by your conscience—then what is your defense against that tactic?

Your best defense is the good news of Jesus. The gospel. The message that promises forgiveness and hope to the browbeaten, that gives peace to the shuddering soul.

And what kind of defense is the gospel? Sometimes the Bible calls it a sword.[33] But is one sword enough to fend off an entire legion of lying, heart-defiling demons?

There is another picture word the Bible uses for the gospel, far more often than it calls the gospel our

---

[33] Ephesians 6:17; Hebrews 4:12; Revelation 1:16; 2:12; 2:16; 19:15,21

sword. Why imagine yourself fending off hell's legion with a sword when you can very properly imagine—no, not just imagine but believe and be certain—that while hell has its legion, on your side is an entire kingdom!

The last contribution to our perspective on demons should include consideration of what the Bible calls the kingdom of Christ.[34]

Actually, we have been talking about the kingdom of Christ from the very first page of this book. In any conversation about the struggle between demons, Jesus, and humans, we are already talking about the kingdom of Christ. And then there is the kingdom of the devil, the kingdom of this world, a kingdom doomed to crumble. The war between these two kingdoms is a hateful and ancient one, a violent series of battles for human souls and human allegiance.

But what I most want you to get your mind around here is this picture: whenever you can apply the gospel to your own heart, there is a holy invasion. There is a storming of the beaches. The kingdom of Christ has arrived, and woe to any unclean legion that tries to drive it back!

---

[34] Synonyms of the phrase *kingdom of Christ* include *kingdom of God* and *kingdom of heaven*. These are different terms but they all refer to the same truth.

The Bible's teaching about the kingdom of Christ has many surprises. The kingdom of Christ is not a place, even though we want to enter it and live in it. The kingdom of Christ is not a thing or a possession, even though Jesus himself tells us to seek it (Luke 12:31). The kingdom of Christ is not a group of people, though the kingdom of Christ is for people. In short, the kingdom of Christ is "not a matter of talk but of power" (1 Corinthians 4:20). Note that. The kingdom of Christ is "a matter of . . . power"! The kingdom of Christ is the powerful, gracious, royal reign of Christ over and for those who trust in him.

What this reign of Christ offers is protection from Satan and peace from all the hatred and grief that Satan stirs up in our lives. Jesus says, "My peace I give you. I do not give to you as the world gives" (John 14:27).

And how this reign comes to people is the gospel.

It may well have been earlier this same day of Jesus' life that we've been studying, I'm not sure I can say definitively, when some of Jesus' enemies accused him of driving out demons by the power and authority of demons (Matthew 12:24). How did Jesus reply? He pointed out how foolish and illogical this accusation was and then said, "If it is by the Spirit of God that I drive out demons, then the kingdom of God has come upon you" (Matthew 12:28). That is to say, because Jesus was in fact driving out demons by the Spirit's power, they all should have realized that this proved that God's power and the holy reign of Jesus had descended from heaven upon earth.

What if we apply those words of Jesus to the exorcism of Legion, which perhaps happened later that very same day? "If it is by the Spirit of God that I drive out several thousands of demons all at once, doesn't that show you that the devil's kingdom is collapsing and that God's kingdom is rapidly conquering it?" Amazing. The defeat of Legion was, then, a display thousands-of-times-over that the kingdom of God was upon them.

This same royal, conquering reign of Jesus floods onto the battlefield whenever and wherever the gospel is proclaimed.

What was the theme of the first sermon Jesus ever preached? "The kingdom of God has come near. Repent and believe in the good news!" (Mark 1:15). How could people be a part of God's kingdom? How could they leave the devil's control? Through the good news, Jesus said. The arrival of Christ's kingdom, the arrival of his good news, and the driving out of Satan are all different ways of looking at one reality.

If we don't understand that King Satan is more afraid of the gospel than of anything else—that good news which brings God's kingdom with great force into Satan's darkest strongholds—if we don't understand how frustrating and fearful that gospel is for him, what a scaredy-cat that makes him, we'll be off guard against Satan's efforts to deprive us of the gospel, its power, and its comforts in any way he possibly can.

Furthermore, if we don't understand that the power which utterly disempowers Satan is the gospel of Christ, we don't understand what our strongest weapon is. We don't understand how joyful it is that we have that weapon. Yes, and may God impress this on your memory: the gospel is not just "a weapon," it is the might and glory of an entire kingdom!

Jesus taught us to pray "Your kingdom come" in the Lord's Prayer. Do you pray that? Do you realize that is a prayer against the control of demons? a prayer for the gospel to come and liberate heart after heart from hell's tyranny?

You are reading that gospel now: the good news of Jesus. The kingdom of Christ is near you. The power of Christ is literally in your hands. Believe in Jesus. Embrace joy and peace. Enjoy rest from conflict. Live in Jesus' light. Rejoice in the Lord always. He is near. "The God of peace will soon crush Satan under your feet" (Romans 16:20).

## Room for Only One King

What country has room for two kings?

There is no room in your heart for both Jesus and demons. That is a tremendously important piece of good news and a superbly comforting promise. Because your heart is full of the gospel of Jesus, because the Spirit has given you rebirth by that gospel, God has made you a new creation who lives for Jesus and whose heart cannot at the same time be controlled or possessed by a demon. It is impossible. You are safe in Jesus' tender care.

James says in his New Testament letter, "Submit yourselves, then, to God. Resist the devil, and he will flee from you" (4:7). No power in all creation can separate you from your Savior. Jesus promises you that no one could ever snatch you out of his hand (John 10:28). And when the roaring lion presumes to afflict you, you can resist him. Take up your shield of faith, the precious Word, the good news of Jesus; and this shield will extinguish "all the flaming arrows of the evil one"

(Ephesians 6:16). Take up Jesus and all of his mighty power, and defeat the devil and all of his demons.

What a King! Praise him for making your heart his own impregnable palace! Praise the Lord with all of your strength and soul! Praise him for keeping you safe. Praise him for delivering you from the devil. Praise him now and for eternity. Praise him.

## Study Questions

Tell about your experiences of the devil using his "favorite tactic" against you.

"The voice that once charmed us now haunts us." What does that quote from the chapter mean? How have you found it to be true?

How can you tell that Jesus has a firm grip on your heart and that you are safe in his tender care? (For help with this question, read the book of 1 John. In this short epistle, the apostle John provides a number of important proofs that demonstrate the presence of an authentic and bold Christian faith.]

Do you ever think of the gospel as your anti-demon weapon? What would be an advantage of thinking that way?

Compare your own past to that of Terry, as told in this chapter. What are some similarities? Differences? Do you find his story more encouraging or discouraging? Explain.

Respond to this reader's reaction to the book: "I think all us Roberts are being unfair to the very real sacrifice that Jesus made for us. Are we skeptical that Jesus went to hell and looked the devil in the eyes and defeated him? No! That was a real thing that happened. And Jesus still protects us from the devil and his demons every day."

List ways that you will be sure to remind yourself every day that you are completely safe in the tender care and powerful protection of your Savior.

Which chapter in the book was most helpful to your perspective on demons? Why?

What could you do to help you remember to praise Jesus every day for protecting you from Satan and his demons? to pray to Jesus every day that he would continue to watch over you and all of his people?

Write a brief prayer that expresses the thoughts and encouragements of this book. Is there someone with whom you might share a copy of this prayer?

# EPILOGUE

*"Then the disciples went out
and preached everywhere, and
the Lord worked with them."*
*Mark 16:20*

How did it turn out for these disciples who had trouble figuring out what kind of man Jesus was? Even after their experience with Jesus on the eastern shore of the Sea of Galilee, they struggled with this question. A key theme in Mark's gospel is that the disciples always struggled with this question, yes, even after Jesus' resurrection. Even when they "got it," they didn't really get it. For example, when Jesus asks, "Who do you say I am?"[35] Peter confesses the truth. He confesses correctly, "You are the Messiah." This seems like progress, but then Peter slips backwards when he rebukes Jesus for talking about suffering death in Jerusalem. Jesus rebukes Peter with that famous reproof, "Get behind me, Satan!" (Mark 8:33).

---

[35] Mark 8:29

Mark's portrayal of Jesus' disciples, though less than complimentary of the disciples, does serve us. In my own relationship with God, I can see that I struggle often to "get it." My heart is hard and I am slow to believe. But Mark's gospel shows me a powerful Savior who never gives up on his disciples. In fact, he took upon himself the punishment his disciples deserved. This is that good news. This is where you and I find our peace, our joy, and wonderful encouragement. The disciples were weak. Our Lord, however, worked with them and in them and through them. We are weak. Our enemies seem powerful. But we work in God's kingdom and under his kingdom; we proclaim his kingdom. His power is near. The Lord works with us and in us and through us.

How will it turn out for you and for me? The devil is still out there. His demons will continue to watch for an opening in our defenses. How will it go for us from here? I will tell you that since I began this project, I have made a few changes in my own life. I have a better perspective. I am still working toward the best perspective. And this new perspective has helped me strengthen my defenses and to improve the outcomes of my life. Specifically, my wife and I always sing a few hymns together just before we go to sleep. We are weary of the secret and hidden attacks of Satan against our hearts. We have largely silenced Satan's attacks and accusations that came in our sleepless hours by filling our hearts and minds with beautiful Christian poetry before we try to go to sleep. It is the Christian poetry that guards our hearts through the night. We pray more. We pray differently. We praise our Lord Jesus for protecting us and blessing us as he has. We praise our Lord Jesus for the seal of triumph he gave us in Baptism and for the regular encouragement he gives us in the Lord's Supper. We think about these things before we go to sleep; we think about what is true, noble, right, and pure. We think about praiseworthy things. It works! It is just a little thing, but it works.

How will your new and better perspective take shape in your life? What are you doing differently to raise your defenses, to stimulate your prayers, and to inspire your praise for Jesus? What are you doing to keep the devil from snatching the good seed that the Spirit planted in your heart? Keep doing those things and know that everything will turn out for us just fine. The kingdom is ours! We pray that God's kingdom keeps coming. We will remain safe and nurtured and encouraged under the royal reign of our King. Our

King tells us how everything will turn out: "Be faithful, even to the point of death, and I will give you life as your victor's crown" (Revelation 2:10).

There is danger and uncleanness all around. There is danger in our own hearts. But by faith in the Son of God, we carry the banner of Christ's kingdom. We enjoy his careful rule over the universe for our benefit. We are not afraid. The kingdom is ours. God's power is ours. Jesus is ours. We are his. That is the way things are right now. That is the way things will turn out.

All praise to you, Jesus. Your kingdom come. Yours is the kingdom and the power and the glory! Amen.

# AFTERWORD AND CODA

What if—God forbid—you were to meet a person who would ask you to pray for a family member suffering from demon possession? What would you say? What would you do?

Let's imagine this scenario in more detail.

Imagine that your confidence in your Savior becomes recognized by people in your various spheres of life. Your unashamed witness of Jesus' mercy and your purposeful Christian life is your trademark. With nowhere else to turn, a coworker approaches you and humbly asks for a few minutes to speak with you in private. Your coworker says, "My younger brother is in trouble. He needs help. We do not know where to turn because all kinds of doctors tell us that there is nothing they can do. The doctors cannot find anything wrong. But something is very wrong."

With that introduction, your coworker goes on to describe behaviors and happenings that lead your coworker to conclude, "My brother has a bad spirit inside him. We need you to come to our home and to pray for him."

This is an extremely difficult scenario. I hope that neither you nor I ever have to wrestle with it. But what could we do to try to help our coworker's family member?

The first thing I would say, of course, is that you need to get together with your own pastors and spiritual leaders to discuss your options, to investigate resources in your community, and to pray for the person whom you have been asked to help. In short, try to get help.

The fact is, help of this nature is going to be hard to find. I asked my pastor-friends who are involved in this ministry for their help. What follows is what they have shared with me to share with you. This is a very short description of what they do when they are called upon to help someone who may be suffering from demon possession.

### Preliminary Preparation

Get to know the family. Some trust would be a great asset in this difficult situation. Determine whether this is a Christian family. Does this family practice a traditional or cultural religion that they brought with them from a different country or community? If this family does engage in a traditional religion, does this religion rely on a shaman, magic, fortunes, spells, or invoking spirits or deceased family members? In other words, is it possible to find out how actively involved the family is in terms of directly engaging the spirit world?

What activities or spiritual practices had the suffering person been engaged in most recently? Had they been exposed in any way to the spirit world? What was the nature of this exposure? Was this person involved in some kind of organized religion that advocated involvement with spirits or demons? Who are this person's friends? What has this person been dealing with in terms of physical sickness, depression, or a spiritual crisis of some kind? Has the suffering person visited places where demons are openly invoked and active?

In other words, my pastor-friends do not go into every situation assuming that there is demon possession. Demon possession is the last option considered. But if there is any kind of history with a direct engagement of demons and spirits, this information may prepare the team for what could follow.

## Preparing the Team for the First Visit

The first thing that a pastor and his "delivery ministry" team will do is to gather together for prayer and Bible study. They will worship together. In this worship time, the delivery team will:

- Read the Bible—Team members will want the strength and confidence Jesus gives through his Word.

- Confess sins and announce forgiveness to one another—A heart full of the assurance of forgiveness is the best protection when facing Satan the accuser.

- Pray for one another, for the family members of the delivery team, as well as for the person they have been asked to help:

  - Ask Jesus for protection.

  - Ask God for direction and for an outpouring of his power appropriate to the suffering person's need.

  - Ask that God's name be glorified through this entire experience.

The delivery team will also review all the details that they have been able to gather regarding the background of the family and person who needs help.

### The First Visit

Assuming that the team will go to the home of the person who needs help, the team will first visit with the family members. Ask them to remain calm. Ask the family to share their fears, concerns, and hoped-for outcomes. Pray with the family. Have a devotion with the family.

Visit with the person who is suffering. Speak directly to the person.

Talk to the person about their own spiritual beliefs.

Pray.

Share a devotion from the Bible that talks about the power of Jesus over demons and the entire universe. Talk about the love of Jesus and how his suffering and death on the cross rescued humans from the devil, death, and the grave.

Ask the person if he or she would like to confess faith in Jesus and to pray to Jesus.

At this point, the team is watching for signs that a demon might be present in the person. These signs would include:

- Unfamiliar voices that the person could not normally use
- Voices that share information or speak in languages that the person would not know
- An unwillingness or strong refusal to say the name of Jesus

- Temperature changes in the room
- Strong and sudden mood changes including intense anger
- Various signs that really cannot be predicted that indicate a supernatural, demonic presence

If there is evidence that a demon could be present, the delivery team would then begin to pray to Jesus and to ask Jesus to remove the evil spirit from the person.

The pastor or delivery team members might say, "In the name of Jesus, get out of (say the person's name)."

Experienced delivery teams report that sometimes the demons leave soon. Sometimes the demons do not leave for a long time. Sometimes the team visits and prays for months before the demons leave. Every case is different.

## Follow Up on the First Visit

It is important to follow up on the entire family. Teach the Christian faith to the entire family. Work to bring the entire family into the fellowship of a loving and supportive Christian congregation where worship and praise of Jesus and Christian living can become the new pattern for the delivered family. Here the family will receive with grateful hearts all of the comfort associated with Baptism and Communion. These special gifts from God will, of course, play a critical role in the family's recovery. When the entire family renounces the devil and his ways and begins a new or renewed relationship with Jesus, the demons will not return.

The delivery team will continue to make visits to pray with the person and their family. The team will pray often for the person and their family. They will keep praising Jesus with this family and praying to Jesus on behalf of this family. When the demons leave, the person and the team will be overcome with joy.

To God alone the glory!

# Learn More About
# This Fascinating Topic

Consider these popular books to deepen
your understanding of this important teaching!